Waking Up as a Bird

Read This Before the Words Expire

VERSES AND PROSE published by
Ladero Press LLC
2763 Lighthouse Cove Road
Orange City, Florida 32763

First Ladero Press Printing, July 2022

Waking Up as a Bird: Read This Before the Words Expire
Copyright © 2022 by Robert Medina
All rights reserved.
ISBNs
978-1-946981-81-3 Paperback
978-1-946981-82-0 EPUB
978-1-946981-83-7 Kindle
Printed in the United States of America
Set in Eb Garamond, and Unna.
Cover Designed by SheerGenius and L.D. Robinson

All rights reserved. The reproduction, transmission, or utilization of this work in whole or in part in any form by any electronic, mechanical or other means, now known or hereafter invented, including xerography, photocopying and recording, or in any information storage or retrieval system, is forbidden without written permission.

For permission, please contact *Ladero Press Editors at* editors@laderopress.com.

The *Verses and Prose* logo is a trademark of Ladero Press.
The *Where Writers Can Soar* logo is a trademark of Ladero Press.

Library of Congress information available upon request.
www.laderopress.com

For my sister Myrna, a true angel on Earth.

Table of Contents

Hidden Phrases 11

Lemmings 13

Different Drummer 15

Gravity 17

The Wedding Dress 18

Pencil and Pen 20

Orchid 21

Somewhere 22

Being Invisible 24

Checking into Heaven 26

Mirage 28

Lost for Words 30

Zoo 31

Solipsism 32

The Barbeque 34

Sternutation 35

DNA 36

Talking to my Friend... What's His Name 37

Lost in the Past 39

I Can See the Forest for the Trees 41

Flat Earther 42

Just Saying..43

What's it Worth...45

Hole 46

Nothing 49

Evening Edition...50

The Persian Rug..52

Thoughts After Happy Hour.......................................53

Light..55

Happy Endings..56

Sheba 59

Phone Call 60

____ 61

Grief Floats in Wine (for Toni W) 62

Extra..63

Under the Covers 65

More About Opportunity 67

Lloyd...69

Would You Recognize God...71

Seagulls...73

Interview with a Ghost at The Myrtles 75

Magic Board..78

Tintinnabulation...79

Half Phrases 80

Symbiotic...81

Waking Up as a Bird 82

Tomorrow 84

Erased 85

After Hours 86

Sequel and Prequel 88

Mundane 91

The Artist 93

Summer Snow 95

Horse Pills..96

The Fate of Words..97

Speed Bump..99

Eight to Five..100

Always Pay Attention to the Details 102

Prodigy...105

Sounds of the Sea...107

Best Night's Sleep of Their Lives.............................109

Nostalgia 110

Little Man 113

Coloring Book (For Dinky) 115

Weighing In 117

More Useless Thoughts About Death (A Dark Ride).....119

Yellow Pencils 121

Flip Books 123

I Have Questions About Clowns 124

Déjà Vu	125
No Stone Left Unturned	127
Language Barrier	129
A Better Place	130
Guest Bathroom	132
Sing for Your Supper	134
Portrait of Bluegills	135
Bookmark	137
Animal Crackers	139
Aquarium	141
Signs	143
Video	144
Palms of Proserpine	146
Happier	147
Trouble with Elevators	148
Creative Juices	150
Blinded by the Light	152
Cheat	153
Levels of Heaven	155
Shopping	157
Strings	158
Empty Dreams	160
Just a Normal Day for a Finch	162
Procrastination	164

Dinner Reservation 166
That's How It Works 168
Resolution 170
Sambuca 171
Hope 173
Bill 175
He Left for Parts Unknown 177
About The Author 178

Hidden Phrases

I suppose that I am like everyone else. I read to be taken somewhere beyond the space I occupy. To be drawn into the words and walk their halls in search of going somewhere new. That is why I read poems; there are hidden roads in poems, pathways that can lead me to places I never imagined were there. I discovered that if I read poems multiple times, I find hidden phrases. Groups of words that are guides to the entrances of avenues that have concealed themselves behind the words on the page.

That's why I like to go back and read again the poems of men and women that I enjoy, even though I have read the same verses two, three, four, or even five times. I do that because sometimes I read it differently. I begin to catch sight of phrases that are acting like shy children. I can see them peeking from behind the words on the paper, and I coax them out by reading them over and over until they trust me enough to finally show themselves. From there, they take hold of my outstretched hand and steer me into a direction that same poem never did before.

There are also those stubborn phrases, ones that are covered inside of a sentence that need to be taken from the page and shaken until they fall from their hiding places. But that can be a good thing because those are usually the ones that bring you to the most interesting doors to open.

So, that's why I read poems more than once to find those hidden phrases that will lead me deep into a poem and take me to places I never anticipated going. Those phrases hold the keys that will unlock gates to a myriad of roads for me to travel. And I'm not at all sure that the authors themselves knew they put them in there.

Lemmings

It began as a beautiful Saturday morning with me headed out toward the beach, the narrow sidewalk acting as an arrow to point the way. It was the first week of spring break, and the entire area was teeming with youngsters who supposedly needed to decompress before finals.

Directly in front of me was a group walking in what looked like a traveling wedge, a human alliance, with one in the front, then two abreast, then three. They were very tight in their pattern. If one of the wingmen should suddenly drop out, it would resemble the missing man formation.

They gave me little notice as we rapidly began to close ground toward each other. Each one had their head down and were deeply engrossed in their phones. They were all right-handed, so the choreography was spectacular. As I approached their position, I worried that if the one in front stopped to let me go by, the rest would all bump into each other and fall like a small set of bowling pins.

To my surprise, the one in the lead cocked an eye my way leaving his device momentarily as if he sensed something was approaching and made an abrupt jaunt to the left. None of the others even looked up but they followed with exact precision. Like a school of fish that suddenly changes directions all at once when the water is disturbed. Or a silent murmuration of starlings shifting their position in the sky as a single intuitive mass. They quickly passed me and continued along on their journey into oblivion.

I stopped to watch them in their singularity, and in that moment, I thought of the metaphor about lemmings. I know there is no truth in the story about lemmings throwing themselves off cliffs to commit mass suicides, but I do believe that if the leader of these young men were to walk off a cliff that happened to be nearby, the entire group would all follow as an ensemble utterly tangled in their devices. I'm sure that they would then be completely and totally unruffled as they tumbled uncontrolled, falling through the air, every single one in unison, and all most certainly texting out selfies the entire way down.

Different Drummer

If He chose to, did you ever consider what musical instrument God would play? I can picture Him sitting in with Tommy Dorsey's Big Band and playing the trumpet, using His jewel crusted wine goblet as a mute.

I tried to imagine Him as a trombone player with Louie Armstrong and his band, but somehow, the vision always came with His long beard being continuously tangled in the chute.

Perhaps He would stand in front of His throne with a large stack of Marshalls on either side, the volume way up, wailing away on a Fender guitar and doing riffs that only God could do. The real rock God.

I've also thought of Him in the traditional sense that one would consider. God, sitting at the end of a large classroom teaching the cherubs how to perform the scales on their harps.

Eventually, I concluded that God doesn't play a musical instrument at all. This occurred to me as I observed my wife at one o'clock in the morning, still wearing her Happy New Year paper hat, empty champagne glass in hand.

There in the silence of our living room, I sat mesmerized as I watched her slowly spin around the floor in her stocking feet, humming a beautiful melody that I had never heard before that night or since.

I know now that we are the instrument He plays, and He is the music. He creates that different drummer that we have heard so much about as we sway to His tune on quiet evenings in living rooms throughout the dance floor's we call life.

Gravity

While standing here on this large sloop, I found myself gathered along with the others, all watching the sun that was directly in front of us slip silently down beyond the edge of the horizon.

I'm not sure why we are always so fascinated with the sunset, something that occurs every day, but tonight the bow of the ship was pointed directly at the center of it, and we were moving full speed ahead in that direction.

It was as if the captain were determined to spear the sun with the front tip of this windjammer so it might drag us over along with it, pull us around to the other side of the earth so that we might see the people on the bottom of the world completely unaware that they are all hanging upside down.

Just a curious thought as we are all of us here on the deck once again, standing straight up and availing ourselves of the opportunity to stare up at a bright and lustrous full moon.

The Wedding Dress

I sat down at a small table in the corner while I was supposed to be assisting a friend whose daughter was soon to be married. Generally speaking, I was the chauffeur and chief package handler. I took my place in the back part of the shop where I was to be out of the way and perhaps taking a short rest from the frantic world of preparing for a wedding.

As I looked around, I noticed that there were several small old tintypes hanging on the wall. One that caught my eye was a portrait of a beautiful young woman who was gazing glumly out into the room from her frame. She, of course, had no smile on her face because that was the custom of the day.

Or, could it be that she wasn't smiling because she received no pleasure in watching so many brides-to-be come in and try on the new elegant dresses of this era. Perhaps her facial expression is there because she is envious of the contemporary styles that she can only and continuously stare at from her place behind the glass.

With that thought in my mind, I believe I may have dozed off for a while. During that time, I envisioned that I had partially opened one eye, and then watched her as she cautiously slipped out of the back of the portrait and began to try on dresses.

I imagined that I saw this young lady holding dress after dress in front of her, slowly twirling herself in front of the full-length mirror. She tried on several until something startled her, and she quickly scampered back into the picture.

I was sure it was just a little dream from my brief nap, that is, until my friend's daughter found something on the rack that she didn't notice before. It was a perfect old-fashioned Victorian style lace dress, exactly the kind that she had been searching for. The odd thing was that it just so happened to have no tags of any kind and wasn't included in the inventory that anyone could find.

Much later, with their business finally concluded and her exquisite dress boxed and in my hands, I went back to the chair to pick up my jacket. As we were about to leave, I saw what appeared to be a small price tag laying on the floor directly below the pictures on the wall where I had been seated. I was going to look up at the tintype as a curiosity but decided not to. I was afraid I might see that beautiful young woman clothed with a modern dress, sitting for her wedding photograph with a huge smile on her face, as is customary today.

Pencil and Pen

When I think about the pencil laying on the desk across the room, I can't help but feel a certain amount of sadness. I think about all the words that are trapped inside of the lead and that so many of those words will never be written. All of them will be lost because the pencil needs to be sharpened.

Too many words will be ground up and tossed aside, never given the chance to tell us their story. That's why I prefer the pen. At least I know each one of those words will get a chance to come out for all of us to read and contemplate.

Every word that I will write in the foreseeable future is contained within this pen that I hold in my hand. They lay there submerged in the darkness of the ink. In time, they will all come out and show themselves on my paper. As for now, I can only wonder what they will say.

I wonder too how many words are inside of this or any pen. I also wonder about the day when this pen runs dry. Out of all the pens there are that can be purchased, how do I go out and find that one specific pen that will contain the words I am supposed to write next?

Orchid

I wonder about you my old friend. Since the decades have passed, I wonder if you are still that free spirit. Still running through those small fields of orchids, spinning along with and in the light of the sun.

Do you still swim like a dolphin barely breaking the surface for a quick breath as you glide effortlessly through the water? Do you still possess that zest for life, one that radiated outward like ripples on a pond, touching anyone that was near?

Are you still doing all of those things, or have you now become a minute part of the orchid in the vase in front of me that sits on the table at this restaurant where I eat alone and wonder whatever became of you?

Somewhere

I am astonished at times by a term that gets bandied about all too often. It is the phrase, "Getting from here to there." I hear it practically every day. No one seems to give a moment's thought about the parameters of the statement before they just blurt it out.

I suppose the time it takes to get from here to there is relative. The distance always changes, but it is nonetheless still referred to as from here to there. The time also changes constantly, but notwithstanding, it continues to be referenced as from here to there. It could take an hour to get from here to there. It could take a minute. It can be used to describe a trip down the block or how long it will take a spacecraft to reach the nearest star.

These postulations are true in every case except when it comes to words. In the time it has taken you to read this, we have both gone from there to here, quite the opposite. But that's neither here nor there. Confused, so am I.

That's the other puzzler that must be woven into this conversation, the expression, it is neither here nor there. Conventional thought tells us that it has to be somewhere. If it's not here, then it must be there, and vice versa. In all the universe, either close by or lightyears away, no matter the time or distance, it most assuredly must be somewhere.

Being Invisible

Looking out from the porch, I watched a bird snatch a bug out of the air that I didn't even see until it was firmly within its grasp. If I didn't know better, I'd swear that bug had been invisible.

I learned today that birds have superb eyesight. According to this reference book that I picked up in the public library to help prove a theory of mine, birds can see ultraviolet and possibly even fluorescent. They can see more images per frame than we can, so basically, I do believe that, like the undetectable bug, if I was invisible, birds could still see me.

While examining my premise, I began to think about the difficulties that would come with invisibility. I'm sure I would get cold running around naked in the winter. If there was a good reason to be unclothed, I'd still have a hard time hiding my cold breath to keep from giving myself away. Imagine the extreme disadvantage one would have if you went to an amusement park and were invisible in the house of mirrors.

Oh, I'm sure there are advantages to being invisible, but there are too many drawbacks to consider. The limitation that puzzles me the most is how do you shave or get a haircut? And when you do cut your hair, does it become visible as soon as the snip is made so one could see it fall to the floor, or does it stay invisible? I hope it would be the latter.

I am certain I would enjoy giving my invisible hairs to birds that I know could see them, to assist in building their nests. I'm sure I'd have great fun watching the astonished faces on those who wonder what's keeping those tiny blue eggs in place that just seem to be hanging there in midair between the branches.

Checking into Heaven

I have always been told that the streets there are paved with gold. I imagine that the shops lining those gleaming streets are sitting on permanent clouds, each one with majestic stairways and grandiose columns.

In one of those shops, there must be an angel who is wrapped in elegant white robes with a tape measure dangling from around his neck. In the rows of chairs lining the eternal halls are his new customers. Each one patiently waiting for a fitting, and of course, time would not be of the essence. While they wait, they browse through catalogs that contain the many different manifestations and styles of wings.

Some will choose a more streamlined model where the tips at the top go beyond the head and then the edges go straight down tucked in tight. Others will select something a little more showy -- short at the top but with great girth. Larger feathers for a fuller look. One at a time, he takes his measurements, and they get to try on several different models until they find the one that suits them. After their fittings, they will have to walk those same lustrous streets until next week when their finished sets of wings will be ready.

Children and babies don't need to stand in line as they will be issued the standard cherub style wings.

Immediately after they are finished, they go to wait again in another building directly across the street. There, the process is much quicker. After all, halos don't require a fitting as they are one size fits all.

Mirage

Yesterday it was extremely hot, even for a day in July. In fact, it was so hot that when I looked out toward the street, I saw the usual materialization of a mirage. There it was, a large and long pool of imaginary water shimmering in the sun.

Later in the day, as the sun slipped into its usual convexity overhead, I noticed that the mirage was gone. There was no doubt in my mind that the imaginary water had evaporated. It had gone back up to those imaginary clouds in the sky that you can never see, the ones that produce mirages.

Today is just as hot as yesterday, maybe even hotter. I looked around to see if I could catch sight of another mirage, but some clouds had paused on their journey and concealed the sun. I had hoped to again see the imaginary water that always floods my mind with unusual thoughts.

For all I know, right at this very moment, some of that imaginary water is spilling out of those imaginary clouds and raining down on top of me, soaking me with its glittering dryness. Flowing like an arid river from the sky. Running down my face and arms to collect into a large and long pool in the street that will be visible once the genuine clouds decide to commence with their travels.

Lost for Words

It seems I have completely lost the idea in just a matter of moments while going from the couch to the desk. I was carrying the idea which I apparently spilled on my short journey to the page. It is gone now.

Some words unseen laying on the floor that will no longer have any relevance because I can't remember what they were. Something that I may never think of again. Something to be swept up by a broom and tossed in the trash.

And it's not as if it hasn't happened before. I imagine there are many thoughts that I lost in the past that have rolled under the desk or have been kicked across the room and lie under my bed only to attempt to force their way back into my head but just get as far as the tip of my tongue.

Some of them may have even become tangled in the paw of my cat which she then ingested while bathing herself and caused her to make that strange guttural noise which sounded something like she was attempting to say, "Found them."

Zoo

It was Monday. Leaning back in the lounge chair in the early morning, a herd of water buffalo came roaring across the sky with the cumulus clouds.

On Wednesday, it was a white rabbit with very large ears that bounced in from the blue with the cirrus clouds.

Thursday, there was an elephant with even larger ears that strolled by, his feet partially covered by the cumulonimbus clouds.

Friday, it was a giraffe that was being slowly followed by a giant turtle and a polar bear, all appearing in tandem from the stratus clouds.

It's Sunday. There isn't a cloud in the sky. I guess that today the zoo is closed, and all the animals are resting in their enclosures hidden somewhere in the sky.

Solipsism

If you have never heard of the word solipsism it is because I did not want you to. That is correct, I did that. I will explain.

Last evening while attending a social gathering for the literary crowd, the topic of solipsism came up within a group hovering around the champagne and pate. There are varying philosophical opinions about the subject that run the gamut from Descartes to Berkeley. Basically, it means that nothing exists outside of one's own mind. That everything which may or may not exist does so within the singular mind of each or even one lone individual. After listening to arguments flying back and forth through three very potent Crown and Cokes, I claimed it was me.

As expected, my declaration was a surprise to those who started and were continuing to have the discussion. I just attested to them that everything in existence was a product of my mind and mine alone. That the universe, this planet, and everyone and everything in it or on it, including the blond woman double dipping the caviar, is solely because of me. Everything that has ever happened in history is my doing. Even the very discussion that was taking place was because I made it happen. You who are reading this right now are only able to read this because you exist as a subtext in this world that I have created inside of my balding but fertile noodle. That was my statement to them.

Of course, my revelation was greeted with laughter and a bit of snickering as expected. But what if I were correct and at that very moment, I suddenly died? Since they exist singularly within my mind, I would have, at the very least, had the pleasure of seeing their stunned faces when everything and everyone that I fabricated, quickly compressed into a small dot that vanished into nothingness.

And if I'm wrong about it being me, if I am not the one, maybe it's you, the person reading this right now. Maybe everything that exists is all in your mind instead of mine. That you are the reason I do, or if you believe the philosophers, do not exist outside of your inventive little noggin.

But if I am the one, I presume that I can make anything become possible. Then again, I think we should keep in mind that all of this could just be in my head, or yours.

The Barbeque

You can always tell when Superman is about to make his entrance to the barbeque. There is a sonic boom immediately before he lands holding a warm Dutch oven filled to the brim with Mrs. Kent's delicious baked beans.

The Human Torch is already there taking care of and making sure the coals are hot and ready to go. The Flash just got back after I sent him to the store because I forgot the tomatoes. I only asked a second ago.

Wolverine is over there cutting up the veggies for the potato salad. He is having a conversation with Storm. She is always a blessing to have over because we know the weather will be perfect.

Aquaman always brings the freshest fish. He likes to roast them over the fire at the end of his trident. It is quite the performance. Bruce Wayne is here sipping his drink and looking bored while he waits for the hamburgers to be done.

Sometimes, I truly feel sorry for Bruce. He has no real powers like the rest. He just sits brooding over there by himself, always looking up to the sky as if he were searching for something.

Sternutation

I pray it is over very soon. It's not that I wish to die, but I'm not sure how much longer I want to live like this. It started when I was a baby. I would make toys move toward me and even roll the bottle across the floor and into my hand.

When I was a young boy, I would amuse myself by making my bike ride all by itself. As I got older, I once hiccupped and caused a small earthquake. There was a time in my forties when my cough created a minor tsunami.

Now I live a very lonely and quiet life, far away from everyone and everything. I do this because of the knowledge that something as simple as a sneeze from me could shift its orbit and change the rotation of the moon or even the earth.

DNA

I am a composite of everyone that came before me. Particles of lint stuck to the fabric of my life. All that each of them did and saw and were, are part of what makes me, me. Pieces of previous lives are woven into this cloth. Bits of them continuing their life inside of me. Fragments of my ancestors are hiding in my legs or my eyes or even my fingers. Minute parts of relatives I never knew reside within me.

I think of this as I stand here today looking out across the fields in old Mexico where my father's fathers father once stood and was witness to what could possibly be the same exact sight. It was then that I felt a sudden tug in my index finger urging me to point, as if it remembered something all by itself.

Talking to my Friend... What's His Name

On my morning walks down the path across from the beach, I am blessed with the ability to write down in my head anything I think is noteworthy. Anything that I may want to bring home and render out onto the page, as I am doing now, usually stays with me. Normally, I can remember it all word for word no matter how long I've been gone.

I am telling you this because you know we have met before, and you just told me your name again, but I can promise you that by the time I turn around to say hello to the person that just walked in the door, I will have forgotten it.

I don't know why, but it only happens with names. It's as if there is a deep well that was dug over time right in front of me, and that names just seem to fall into it. A hole that was bored out and given a slippery edge so that when you and your name come over to shake my hand, your name slides off down the slope and breaks up as it crashes into all the other names at the bottom of the pile.

One day not long ago, I decided to take all the broken names out of the hole and place them on a table. It was like a huge jigsaw puzzle, and I was going to reassemble the letters, put a face with a name as it were. I have never been good at putting puzzles together, so I may have forced a few pieces where they weren't supposed to go. What I'm trying to say is, if I get your name wrong, please don't hold it against me . . . Larry . . . Jim . . . sorry . . . is it Andy?

Lost in the Past

I pinched that line from a writer. "Lost in the past." I thought of those four words when I literally ran into her as she came from around the corner of a building, just as she did in the opposite direction when she disappeared from my life long ago. In barely an instant, those four words entered my mind which then set in motion the interlocking gears that began turning again. The pieces of rust quickly broke off, and our past became a smooth operating machine in my mind.

Until that moment, I had always thought of her as just that -- lost in the past. That she somehow never changed. I pictured her as being caught up in something back in that time and that she remained exactly as I remembered her. My mind always dismissed the reality that it had been so many years and that her looking different was inevitable.

I mean, it's not as if, when she vanished around that corner, she was somehow guided into a labyrinth of time, keeping her exactly as she was. It's not as if she has been wandering around through this maze of tall green hedges for decades, unable to escape. It's not as if, should I see her again, she will not have aged, not even a moment.

All of this ran through my mind in a flash as she smiled at me with the same smile I knew and looked into me with those same haunting blue eyes. All of this rushed through my head immediately before I began helping her pluck what looked to be the leaves of a hedge out of her hair.

I Can See the Forest for the Trees

I can see the electricity as it pours out of all the tiny holes from the outlets in the walls and then out onto the cold floor but I can't help the bits of energy I see all scrambling to climb over one another while attempting to get back inside of the warm wires.

I can see the crack that forms in the ground behind me whenever I am walking and then cross over the border from the sunlight and into the shade but I can't do anything as I watch my shadow slip into that crack and listen to its silent screams as it falls away into the darkness.

I can see the ugly words that leave people's mouths and travel on the air like unsavory hitchhikers but can do nothing to deflect them before they are picked up by the ears of others.

I can see and I can feel the world constantly and continuously turning beneath my feet but I can't run fast enough in the opposite direction for it to seem like I am ever standing still.

Flat Earther

As I sit here in my pajamas sipping a fresh cup of Kona, I am reading a story about those who believe the earth is not a ball such as the globe sitting on the desk across the room, but is, in fact, flat. A pancake poured in the sky. A map rolled out onto the table of space. A thin page torn from the atlas of the universe. A giant wink without a tiddly.

One fellow in the article genuinely believes it to be true. He is so certain he and the others are correct that he is going to take a trip. It will be an expedition of sorts that will bring them to the virtual ends of the earth, or in their minds, the actual end of the earth. He wishes to walk to the outer perimeter and prove once and for all that it is there.

I would love to take that trip to the arctic with them. When we reach the edge, it would be interesting to watch as a cosmic wind came along and snapped off some of the huge dangling icicles that must be tenuously attached to the fringe. We could all peer over the lip and watch them fall through space, creating new craters in the flat landscape of the moon.

Just Saying

Never in my life have I ever had a bird in the hand, with the possible exception of a small parakeet perched upon the end of my finger, but I would have to believe that that would not be considered as in the hand. I have seen two birds in a bush, and sometimes as many as four, but I suppose because there was just the one bush, they felt obligated to share.

There are probably very few circumstances that one might be able to think of where doing it late is better than never doing it at all. Maybe if you are late for a movie, depending upon just how late, it may not be worth doing at all. If the plot hinges on the opening moments, skip it. After being late for class on numerous occasions, my teacher remarked that I would one day be late for my own funeral. That is undoubtedly something I would rather be so late for that I would love to skip it altogether.

I never set out to save pennies, it just sort of happened. I tossed a few into a jar one day that had been jangling around in my pocket and kept right on doing it. I would have to say that very few of them were earned. Most were found. There would be Lincoln staring up at me from edge of the sidewalk or on the black contrast of a parking lot, so I'd pick him up and later slip him into the jar to stare at all the other likenesses of himself. Not much can be done with a jar of pennies today, but if I ever need someone's thoughts, and as I understand it, the going price is a penny each, I believe I have enough to pay for quite a bit of counsel. I would like to say that this is food for thought, but that would be encroaching upon a whole different matter that has something to do with a meal never being free.

Sometimes, I would find one in a drawer. Other times, I would find a displaced one in the closet on the floor. There would, of course, be the occasional one rattling around in an old cigar box or tucked away safely inside of my grandmother's fancy church coin purse. I found some that were round and some that were square, some shiny and some that were dull. I have seen hundreds, maybe thousands. I have seen some that were attractive, some lovely, and even a few that were appealing. But despite my continuing search, which includes the scores that turned up in my mother's sewing box, never in my lifetime thus far, never have I ever found a button that I would remotely describe as cute.

What's it Worth

One day, I am going to get a pen and paper and begin with whatever character comes to mind: a pigeon, a woman or perhaps an aardvark.

Then with great patience and ultimately some extreme personal skill, I will draw a picture that, if one studies it while standing across the room, it will look exactly like my subject is supposed to look, and with such stunning detail, that any onlooker would have great difficulty discerning it from the real thing.

But if that same observer were to cross the room and get very close, they would find that I perfectly executed this likeness using only words, all flawlessly strung together and spaced to create my picture. Only words. And to be exact, only a thousand of them.

Hole

There was a lightning storm last night. I coincidentally peered through the curtains and out of the window just in time to witness a bolt striking the huge tree outside in the front yard. I felt its power through the room, and there was the lingering odor of an electrical charge in the air.

As the next morning came around, I went out to assess the damage. What I found was that the tree was perfectly intact except for a small dark hole about the circumference of my index finger. It was exceptionally round. I slid my finger into it as if it were a key and turned it slightly. The hole moved. Left to right, up and down, in circles, it shifted to any point I chose.

I pulled my finger out and the hole hung onto it. I couldn't see the half of my finger that was still inside of it. As perplexed as one might normally be, I did not panic but carried it inside the house. I sat down at my writing desk and placed my finger on the top of it. The hole fell off and my finger was free. I could now look down into the hole and see what was inside of the top drawer surrounded by a hazy area of darkness.

I placed my finger back inside and pulled the hole to the edge of the desk. It then fell and landed on my shoe. I could see my toes moving around as the hole itself became a little bigger and the surrounding darkness also increased. I picked the hole back up and played with it for a while looking into various things. It was odd to see the inside of an inflated football and not have it lose any air.

I needed to go out to the storage shed so I took the hole with me. It began to expand and become heavier so I flung it off my finger, and it stuck to the bottom of the wall. When it landed in the corner, it startled a small mouse that quickly ran inside of the hole. I looked in but didn't see him, just darkness now. I don't know where he went. It was at that point that I decided to put the hole back on the tree where it all started. I had deemed it far too dangerous to continue what I was doing.

As I dangled it out to attach itself to the tree, it was considerably larger than when I started. Shortly after that, I watched a bird land on its edge and go inside the hole in the tree. It too disappeared. This all happened last week. Since then, it has continued to grow ever larger and much faster than before.

The tree is gone now as is everything that surrounded its edges. The hole continues to grow larger and deeper every hour with it devouring anything it touches. Overnight it engulfed enough land around me to cut off any escape from this place. It's just a matter of time before it swallows up everything in this circle, including me. All I can do now is watch. The only thing that I know for certain is that very soon I shall find out what happened to the mouse and whether or not that bird can fly above what's on the other side of the hole.

Nothing

Today I wanted to write about nothing. Writing about nothing is not easy. Everything is something so writing about nothing becomes complex. When it comes right down to it, there is nothing that is nothing or anything that could be considered nothing. Nothing is supposed to be an empty space, a void, a cavity, but all of them are actual things. There is no void without something around it that can help define it. That's the only way you can see nothing. And even then, even when you see nothing, it's still something even though it is nothing. So today, I was going to write about nothing, but nothing really came to mind.

Evening Edition

I get the newspaper like most. All of the so-called news that's fit to print arrives in my driveway early in the morning, delivered by some mysterious unseen four wheeled conveyance in the dark of the predawn hours.

It all sounds normal, but here's the thing: I started getting the evening edition in the morning. That's right. News of what will happen later in the day is stuffed inside of that thin little piece of plastic bag that comes daily to my driveway.

It has happened now three days in a row. The first day, it was just an odd surprise, maybe a joke, I thought. The second day, I checked to be sure, and what I had before me was the numbers for the lottery. I had the scores of games I could bet on and get rich overnight.

That was yesterday, and I'm sure the numbers will be correct again for today. But at this point, I find myself not so interested in that as I am another bit of news.

Earlier, while I was fantasizing about my mansion or what island I would buy, I stumbled across my name in the obituary section. So right now, I am just sitting here waiting for what happens next, realizing that unless they notice, someone in my family will be stopping my subscription very soon.

The Persian Rug

It was strolling through the French Quarter in New Orleans that started this whole fantasy, a store on Royal Street that sold vintage rugs to be precise. A place where I purchased a centuries old rug made in what is now modern-day Iran. I brought it home and rolled it out onto the wooden floor, and that is where my daydream began.

It started with me, gliding down from above the buildings in the city. I climbed off, and it hovered next to me at an outdoor Magazine Street restaurant. I believe something Arabic would have been appropriate for lunch. After that, we took to the clouds and finally floated in through the front door, sliding into the position it holds at this moment. I took this fantasy with me when I went to bed for the night.

In the morning, I noticed that one edge of the rug was flipped and turned over onto itself. I would love to blame it on the cat, but my heart wants to consider something else. It wants to believe that the rug was indeed a magic carpet but over time had used up all its power. I envisioned a rug that lacked the strength to carry anyone for some time, but now that it has been set free from the pile of rugs, it had attempted one last flight with what little magic it had left.

Thoughts After Happy Hour

Have there ever been two kernels of popcorn that have popped and looked completely and totally identical?

What if rain was not round drops but fell in squares? Would puddles be square?

Why is it that I can still see evaporated milk?

How do we know when the letter X is accidently printed upside down?

If a dog's life is seven to our one and you leave him for eight hours to work, for him, does it seem like fifty-six?

"When one door closes, another one opens" should only apply to revolving doors.

Strawberries are not made of straw; blueberries are not really blue; and don't get me started on grapefruit.

If I deflate the air from a football and put it into a basketball, will it bounce funny?

Are elderberries the oldest berry?

Why does a quarterback play the entire game, a halfback plays three quarters of the game, and a fullback plays a quarter of the game?

When hot chocolate cools off completely, is it now just chocolate milk?

If you were to pour disappearing ink onto camouflage, what the hell would happen?

If one actually did have ice water in their veins, can you imagine how cold iced tea would seem to them?

The letter Q is just an O with a kick stand.

moving down a path from screen to screen into a world of non-stop happy endings.

Shortly after this screen went dark, I could picture him as he entered a new one filled with sunshine and fresh air, where he stopped by a fence and handed a few sugar cubes to Flicka right before she returned to again run carefree around the open field. He then wandered down that trail and to the next where he stepped off the path and into a screen to check on Lassie since he heard she had just come home. After a few playful licks, he bid them all goodbye where he casually continued over the upcoming hill and then made his next entry, arriving just in time to witness Dorothy and Toto being taken home by virtue of the magic contained in her ruby slippers. Following that cheerful moment, he departed the Emerald City, traveling out and along his own Yellow Brick Road, going in a direction where Dorothy and her companions had never been.

Sometime later, he crossed into a scene with a snowy street where he was invited to an impromptu party being thrown for George Bailey. He stood in the back of the room singing with the others including George's brother Harry who had just flown in that night through a blizzard. Even though it was continuing to snow heavily, he said, "Goodnight!" and left them all, walking with that step still in his gait as he jaunted off down another road. A road, that in my ongoing vision, will blissfully extend itself out in front of him for as long as movies have happy endings to visit.

And that's where I picture him now, right where we left off: looking out through the snow where he can see what he believes to be an outline formed by the back of a large wooden wardrobe protruding from a grove of snow-laden trees and being guarded by what appears to be a lion.

Sheba

They say that curiosity kills the cat. I'm not exactly sure how it does, but I would hate to bear the responsibility of bringing any harm to mine simply because she is curious about something and I cannot provide her with an answer.

She is getting on in years, and I'm sure that she has found many things over time that have confused her. I wish I could explain to her that there is a reason and a purpose for the vacuum cleaner which she despises.

I wish she could understand that it would bring her harm if I were to acquiesce and give her some of the chocolate she seems to want so desperately whenever she happens by while I am eating some.

I wish I could explain to her that she came to us as a rescue with no claws and that is the reason she cannot go outside and perhaps interact with another cat who could brandish weapons if an altercation took place.

With her advancing age, I know there are many things she wants to ask. It's plain to see in those eyes that stare at me for hours on end. The ultimate giveaway is when I say, "Sorry . . . no" and she stands by me with her tail taking the form and shape of a question mark.

Phone Call

I am sitting across the room as she is talking on her phone. At times, the conversation seems to be quite humorous. Other times, it takes on a more serious tone. Right now, there seems to be an emphatic argument taking place.

I guess, that in her mind, the prattler on the other end is making no sense. I gather that by the way she is stopping at times to just shake her head in disbelief. Her hand gestures give me the impression that she has become frustrated with the conversation right before she hangs up. She then storms out of the room mumbling something unintelligible.

I hope that perhaps the party she has been conversing with on the other end has someone sitting across the room from them, too. Someone who is also trying to comprehend the diverse conversation that was taking place, only from the other side. I wish I could pick up the little pink toy phone, now that she is through, and talk to that onlooker. I would love to have a counterpart on the other end of the world she's created who could lift that imaginary phone, place it to their ear, and explain to me the complicated verbiage that generously flows from the mouth of a two-year old.

This poem has no title. It has nothing to help guide you. Nothing to trigger something in your mind for you to follow, a word or two to point out the path that you believe you will go down.

No idea for you to start with. Nothing to trip a switch for a spotlight to cut through the darkness and send you in a certain direction. Nothing to be that first push that makes the dominos fall in a broken line.

No breadcrumbs to follow along a trail out of a forest of words leading you into the light beyond the sentences. It has no beginning, and in the end, it will only be about what you think it's about.

Grief Floats in Wine (for Toni W)

I came upon a sound in the brush. It was a writhing sound, a sound of distress. Something was struggling there in the woods next to the clearing.

When I got to the edge of the trees, I saw what I thought was a deer caught in a trap. As I got closer, I realized that it was not a deer but the shadow of a deer caught in a steel trap with the deer standing close by looking very concerned at us both.

I got down to the ground and attempted to calm it down. Searching around, my hand found a thick branch. I pushed hard on the release mechanism; the shadow got its leg out as the trap snapped back empty.

When I looked up, I saw the shadow quickly running off into the deep woods along with the deer, both of them limping.

Yes, it was a silly dream but not as silly as attempting to rinse away my grief by uncorking a couple of bottles of dark pinot then falling asleep while sitting out here on the swing by the woods, just me and my shadow.

Extra

They are in every cowboy show on television and in every western themed movie. There is always at least one. The lone guy sitting out in front of the bank or the general store, his chair leaned back against the wall. His arms are folded, and his hat is pulled down over his eyes as if he were taking a nap.

I always wondered about him. Who is he? Does he have a home, and is he just stealing some quiet time away from the Mrs.? I don't know anything about him except that he is as integral a part to the show as the saloon and the bank and the stables, the hitching posts and the dirt streets.

He helps bring the mood to a show. Much like the older couple in their finest dress leaving the bank or the shopkeeper outside with his broom, sweeping the wooden sidewalk in front. He is just as important as the others walking by the blacksmith's shop while he is out there sweating in his apron and pounding a horseshoe.

If the solitary sleeping cowboy wasn't there, the scene would feel as if a part were missing. Like a stagecoach without someone riding shotgun or a herd of cattle without someone yelling, "Stampede!"

So I salute you, cowboy, sleeping in a chair. Man who is always there. Man who is not listed in the credits. Man making the whole experience seem complete.

Under the Covers

Tonight, as I peeked in to check on the child of a friend that I had been charged to watch this evening, I found he was under the covers with the new book I had given him. The softened glow coming from beneath the sheets brought back memories of the light pouring out from the end of my flashlight, spilling and splashing all over the front of a book, just as it did practically every night of my childhood. It fed the words on the cover like seeds that sprouted, and I watched as tangled vines grew to form a cave that surrounded me.

I would open the book, and the power that came from deep within the magic wand in my hand would spark a kindling of words and start a blaze that would roar across the turning pages. They would become a torch that illuminated the stories within. I used that torch to start a campfire before I used it once again to enter the dark passageways inside the books. It gave my friends a light to follow so they could reach me.

It led them all to a place where characters could emerge from their books, sit around and warm themselves next to the fire. A shelter for dragons, elves and hobbits to climb out from the hallways of ink and rest around me. It was a haven for every type of creature to gather, even the occasional beautiful maiden. A safe setting for them to tell their enchanted tales and adventures to me and to each other.

After a while, we would all fall off to sleep together where they would enter my dreams. Dreams that I shared as a place for them to live out their fantasies. At last, a setting for them to make their own dreams come to life.

More About Opportunity

I heard someone say today that they had a window of opportunity that was also a once in a lifetime opportunity, and now, I'm trying to understand the diverse abilities that opportunity has been known to employ when presenting itself.

First, I must ask how did that individual know the window was even there? Could it be that it got his attention because he heard opportunity knocking, but this time, directly on the window? I always assumed, as most do, that when opportunity knocked it would be on the door. But I suppose one could never be sure as it seems that occasionally opportunity prefers to use a window.

And although he wasn't very specific, one would also think that it would probably be easier for that person to take complete advantage of opportunity if the window were open. One could certainly rationalize that opportunity would be much harder to get to if the window were closed.

I would think it would be entirely within reason to assume that it would be even harder if you were outside of the window and that window was locked from the inside while opportunity was waving and tapping on the glass, looking out at you from the other side. If you had to break the window of opportunity to get in, would that hurt your chances?

That brings me to the last of these senseless thoughts: what if opportunity came knocking and was unfortunate enough to randomly knock at deaths door? I have my own opinion on the matter based on the history of opportunity as we know it. My guess is that death would seize the opportunity right then and there, and that would, in fact, be the reason that at least for death, opportunity would only knock once.

Lloyd

Very few of you that read this will have ever known Lloyd. A man who lived until just a couple of weeks shy of turning one hundred years of age.

He was a man with a handshake that would have had the envy of any vise grip. A man with an enormously large heart. The affection he showed to those he loved, and to even strangers like me, must have taken up half of those years.

A man that death passed by so many times because it was afraid of having to deal with the struggle it would most certainly find in such an irascible spirit. Death reasoned it was to its own advantage that it was better off waiting until he was worn down by time.

And what makes up a hundred years, a century, a number we like to affix as a milestone? Lloyd certainly knew. I always believed that he thought of it as a hundred miles strung out over a road that bends beyond the distance that we can see in front of us. A journey that very few get to complete.

He accomplished it by crawling across childhood then walking through distant valleys trying to evade becoming a wartime casualty. Managing to slip around death without being noticed, cheating it from turning him into just a few lines in a telegraph.

From there, it was a slow jog, embracing and appreciating the scenery. Spending decades running far ahead of death and pulling away without really trying. He also pulled a forest worth of pages from calendars exclaiming to everyone that he would live to be at least a hundred, and likely more.

Right now, Lloyd is probably threatening death, pissed because he let death tiptoe up on him just shy of his objective. Somewhere out there, he's sitting on death's back and has him in a choke hold, laughing out loud in his boisterous voice all the while preventing death from sneaking up on someone else. Making sure that person will reach their goal while death is forced to watch as he himself is pinned to the floor, gasping for air.

Would You Recognize God

How would He appear to us? Would He be the supreme being in gold flowing robes sitting upon a majestic throne coming down from the sky floating on an abundance of clouds saturated with spiraling tubes of hallowed light?

Maybe it would be something more subtle. Perhaps He could be the old man with the silvery white beard and piercing blue eyes standing on the street corner handing out brochures that say, "PRAY."

Or maybe, He would be the child that I can see this morning across the playground in the park, blowing on the scraped knee of a little girl whom I assume is his sister, wiping her tears and telling her everything will be alright.

Maybe He's the tiny baby in the open carriage parked next to his mother, the one with the huge smile that brings even more smiles from everyone who leans down to let him grip tight and shake their fingers.

Maybe He's the golden retriever whose tail is constantly wagging and can't seem to get and give enough love from all those passing by as he sits anxiously on his leash waiting for more strangers' attention.

Perhaps He is the bird that I can't see but can hear that is elegantly entertaining everyone here with his bright tune bringing joy as it wafts through the air on this most spectacular day.

Or maybe, He is the ant I see by my feet carrying the partially eaten crust of pizza dough that is probably hundreds of times its weight, which to me seems like an impossible burden that only God could manage.

Seagulls

If you ask anyone who knows me, they will tell you that I am not someone you would confuse with an artist, but I do still enjoy painting. My lack of skill is countered by my ability to paint more into the picture than most, a special gift that I have been given. The latest case in point: last week, I painted a picture of a seagull standing on the beach.

It has dried while sitting on an easel in the den. Right now, it looks to be just the bird, the beach and the sea. But if you consider the fact that I am capable of painting beyond the painting, I'm certain that in the sea there are fish that I painted so the seagull might have the opportunity to eat. Also, directly under the surf, there are a large variety of shells that I placed right below the water's surface.

To the left of the frame, just out of sight from anyone that might be standing in the room and trying to appreciate the picture, there are other seagulls sitting on posts at the dock where boats are tied up. I put them there barely out of sight to give my lone seagull some company.

This morning, when the den was empty and no one was around, I thought I heard them all flapping about, scurrying along the beach squawking at each other. As per the norm, when someone approaches the room, they all fly back to their places out of frame, and they wing their way back to their normal positions in the painting. That's the problem with being able to paint like this. After a few weeks, most of my art looks to be pretty much empty and lacking any content.

And yes, as always, I do expect that one morning soon, I will wake up and find that the lone seagull -- tired of holding his place in the portrait -- has flown off with the other gulls leaving me with just another amateurish deserted beach scene like the ones before.

I sometimes wonder where they go to when they go elsewhere in my painting. Perhaps right now they are being fed by some children who are tossing Cheetos up into the air for them to catch. Probably in front of a place just a little farther down from the soon-to-be-empty beach scene, right past the boat house I painted in there at the last minute much farther out of anyone's sight.

Interview with a Ghost at The Myrtles

Through my visiting this place many times, I have come to appreciate the spirits that dwell here. Of course, they don't have a room or a bed. No bathing facilities to utilize. They don't raid the ice box late at night. But they are here for some reason, and I asked one if I might have an interview to see exactly what it is that keeps them around. He enters. The room turns chilly. Here is our conversation.

Me: What's your name?
Him: What difference will it make.

Me: OK . . . did you die here?
Him: Yes.

Me: How did you get from the cemetery back to the house?
Him: I never left . . . was just the body that left.

Me: Was it your soul that stayed behind?
Him. Something like that.

Me: How did you die?
Him: I was shot.

Me: Why?
Him: Pardon the pun, but it's not worth reliving.

Me: In the movies, they say ghosts stay behind because they have unfinished business. Do you?
Him: I don't know what that means, but it has something to do with everything I did wrong in life. I'm stuck here without the ability to leave, plus I can't taste or smell or touch.

Me: But you can move things?
Him: I can move things, but I can't feel them.

Me: How long do you think you'll be here?
Him: I'm not exactly sure. It seems that I must pay a price for what I have done and am being punished until they feel like it's enough.

Me: Who are they?
Him: You tell me.

Me: Have you ever said, "Boo!"
Him: (Laughs) No.

Me: Is there an afterlife?
Him: I'm not sure, but I'm here now, aren't I?

Me: Do you have the sensation of passing time?
Him: Yes, but for some reason, it's a lot slower than it used to be.

Me: Why do you think people are afraid of you?
Him: I think it's because they fear what they can't explain. I hope doing this interview will help.

Me: One last thing: can you tell me how to do that turning a room instantly cold trick? That could come in handy.
Him: Ever hear the expression, "I will take that to my grave?"

Me: Yes . . .
Him: That's one of those things you find out when you get here.

Magic Board

I found it on the floor this morning. It is a rectangular black magic board that you can write on with a stylus and is used to help those of us with poor memories. I keep it to make lists of things for the grocery store. I then only need to push a button, and the words are magically drawn inside of it and disappear into a void.

I've had it for years. By now, there should be stacks of words like bread, milk and water everywhere inside. Columns of the words wine, cheese and juice have been crammed in there over time. Of course, there would be the occasional nine-volt battery shoved back into the corner by itself.

At first, I thought perhaps the sticky tape that kept it on the wall had given out but since the board no longer works, I am now inclined to believe that there are just so many words packed into it that it has reached its capacity. Its being on the floor is just the result of the over-crowded words pushing against the blank surface from the other side.

Tintinnabulation

I saw that the old upright piano had been placed outside of the school to be hauled away. Left to settle by the side of the road, it lay there on its back with the music wires exposed. Its once many keys are now mostly cracked and largely missing. It seemed an unfortunate and unfit end to something that was so alive for so very long.

In that moment, the air grew very still and quiet as if offering a gesture of reverence to the piano. It then grew dark and began to softly rain. As it did, the drops struck the bare strings inside to play a song written by the heavens. It didn't sound like a cacophony as you might expect, but instead, a quiet knell befitting the death of the music.

Half Phrases

I love half phrases. If I were to say to someone that I was half-dressed, which half would it be? The top half or the bottom? The left or the right?

If I said I have a half a mind to do something, would I only do half of what I wanted to do, and by the way, what would the other half of my mind be doing all that time?

But that's not the half of it. If you won half the battle, don't you think it might be appropriate to make a sincere effort to win the other half?

If you taste your drink and say to yourself, "That is not half bad," would you prefer the glass to be half empty or half full of that drink, and was that drink cheap at half the price?

Of course, none of this has ever been meant to be literal. No one could ever actually run all over hell's half acre or keep half an eye on something.

For if it were, and I said to you right now that I am writing this half-heartedly, I would have to keel over from my chair, half-dead from the whole experience.

Symbiotic

It was a brief excursion. I quick getaway from the madness of the city to Chankanaab State Park in Cozumel. A boat took us out to the reef so we might have a relaxing hour of snorkeling. It wasn't long before I spotted a small tomato clownfish that was nestled inside the tentacles of a sea anemone.

Those same tentacles shoot off tiny harpoons into their prey, which includes many other species of fish that the anemone finds tasty, but not the clownfish. He sits there completely unaffected and unharmed. His bright colors attract prey for the anemone, and in return, he is protected from prey of his own.

How nice it would be if I could do the same within my world. I would so love to be able to walk through the groves of rose bushes that I grow here in the expanse of the backyard and be totally unaffected by their thorns. To never be pricked by the plants that I nurture and feed.

To be able to sit there on the ground, wrapped inside of them, immune from those who might come too near. To be shielded from harm by anyone. And if I could, I would just stay there long enough for the roses to bloom around me and hide me altogether.

Waking Up as a Bird

I would love to awaken one morning and find that I was a bird. To open my eyes and see the droves of branches surrounding me, to hear the rustling of leaves as the high wind passes through them.

To look down, and with some trepidation, let go of the limb where I stand and take that first cautious step into the expanse of nothing that stretches out beneath my claws.

To anxiously spread my wings and feel what it's like to take flight. To soar. To ascend above the trees and then easily glide down, land, and sit upon the fence I had constructed around my house.

I would hop over to the bright red birdhouse that I built last winter and see it from a whole new perspective. I'd eat from the feeder that I topped off just yesterday and bathe in the birdbath I filled with fresh water the day before that. I would converse with the other birds that I normally must view, for fear of scaring them off, from my kitchen window.

I would flutter over and perch myself upon the sill to peer into the bottom of the living room window. I would watch through different eyes as my wife stands next to the couch trying desperately to wake me.

Tomorrow

The sign outside of the bar says that tomorrow there will be free beer. Of course, the joke being that tomorrow never comes. Tomorrow is that elusive place where the weather, without exception, is always going to be perfect for you.

A place where you can sit at a small table out in front of your favorite tavern and enjoy the moment without worrying about what is to come because it never will. Next door, there is a little shop where you can sample endless opportunities you are certain that you deserve.

Directly across the street is another store where possibilities are free to you for the asking. A place where people will walk by, smile and hand you boxes of great things to come and bags full of riches that you believe, in your procrastinating little heart, are completely justified.

Tomorrow is a location where you always seem to feel at home. Yes, tomorrow is a place where the beer is always cold, and the beer is always free.

Erased

Closing the refrigerator door, I just happened to glance at the magnetic board that was stuck to it. The board that contains a list of names and numbers that we occasionally call on the phone, all written in erasable black marker. At the very bottom of that list was the name of a cousin that passed away last year.

It made me think about how many lists I may be on, hanging from refrigerator doors or on a typed page pinned to a note board somewhere. And one day I'll be that guy, the name someone notices -- then remembers -- that I had moved on from this life, and that my name and number are still there, waiting to be erased.

And one by one, over time, people will eventually erase me from their lists until I have been removed from them all. I do hope that a few will leave my name there as a reminder that we used to talk to each other. Even better, maybe one will forget that I am gone and try to call me. Even better than that, maybe I'll answer.

After Hours

It is Sunday, and I am in the bookstore as usual. The books are also here as usual, any type of book that anyone could possibly want. Books of stories, fiction and nonfiction. Books of history, finance and even those for learning to cook like a southerner are housed here. All perched upon shelves with the eyes of their titles staring out at the people browsing. All of them divided into their unique and individual sections. That is, at this moment.

Last night, when I was driving past this store, I thought I saw some commotion going on inside the darkened windows after everyone had left to go home and the lights were turned out. I would swear that the quiet time may be the signal they all wait for. The moment when the books on birdwatching and ornithology leap from the shelves, open themselves up and with spine down, the pages begin to flap like wings so they might fly freely about the place.

The section where the books about automotive mechanics spring wheels and begin to chase each other around the floors. In the sci-fi area, books brandish lightsabers and begin to battle each other while at the same time, in the romance area, books begin to interlock. Their alternating pages sliding side by side into each other, as if at arms-length, and begin to dance around in circles on tabletops. That is just a tiny sample of what I believe happened here.

Right now, it's just me alone in a small area in the back of the store. I tend to believe that I am probably the only one who thinks something went on last night once it was dark and quiet. That is the reason I am back here in a section that I would normally not find myself. I am here thumbing through this particular group of books, with the expectations that one of them may have captured some evidence on its pages last night. After all, this is the photography section.

Sequel and Prequel

In this time of sequels and prequels I have given some serious thought to two possibilities that would be of interest to me: one is a tale of the heart and another of injustice.

For the first one, I wish someone would do a prequel, the background story of The Scarecrow from *The Wizard of Oz*. The movie would practically write itself. I can see it all it now: the first scene opens with a breathtaking shot, the sweeping expanse of a field of barley waving in the wind.

Then, a wholesome look at his humble beginnings growing up into fine young straw in that field. It would cover his brave childhood where he and his family had to fight off locusts just to stay alive. Then, a scene where we get to witness how he was assembled in the barn of the farmer that grew him.

It would be an amazing saga that chronicles his entire life. It would cover everything up to the climactic moment when Dorothy frees him from his oppressive job to become an independent thinking man of the world. A real feel-good story. Audiences would leave the theatre in tears of joy.

Or, perhaps a sequel would be more interesting. When the story begins, we would find our intrepid Scarecrow in Oz running against the mayor of Munchkinland for the office of Wizard. This film would present dirty politics at its best. During a heated election campaign that contains a great deal of mudslinging, a scandal soon breaks out.

The coroner implicates him in the murder of the Wicked Witch of the West. You can imagine the tense courtroom scenes that are sure to pull at the heartstrings of everyone in the theatre. And of course, without Dorothy there to corroborate his story, he has little chance. After a stressful and lengthy trial, you are spellbound by the impassioned, although high-pitched speeches, given by both the prosecutor and the defense. You're taken inside of the room where the jurors show the conflicted strains of their duty. One of the last holdouts to finally give in is an emotionally tortured member of the Lollipop Guild.

Flash ahead to the foreman delivering their verdict of guilty: he is convicted and sentenced to death along with the Tin Man and the Cowardly Lion. And even though he was a victim of political treachery, we still witness our hero bravely signing his last will and testament, donating his magnificent brain to science, along with his body, which is to be given to the Little Munchkins of the Poor to make brooms for the needy.

He passes on his last meal because, as we already know, he doesn't eat a thing. This movie keeps you on the edge of your seat until the very end.

A tale that is, of course, designed to bring awareness to the supposed problematic court systems and unsavory political backroom dealings throughout Oz. The last scene is a final passing shot of the Scarecrow immediately before his execution that slowly cuts to those in the gallery witnessing his final moments. Fade to black. And once again, not a dry eye in the house.

The Artist

Rising in the late afternoon, he ever so slowly and gracefully crosses the floor and looks out of the window in front of him. His hand moves forward to grasp the bright orange disc: the thing that we call the sun. It is attached to the top of the long gray rod stretched across the visible sky that we know as the horizon.

He creates the sunset as he slowly begins to draw down the shade of the day. Now, with the canvas of night in front of him, he takes a seat on his stool, places his thumb through the wooden hole and brings his pallet up to his side. A pallet with only two colors, deepest blue and brilliant white.

With his brush he begins the long strokes that trace and color in with blue, the path of stars that flame out as they shoot across the sky. He then adds new bright white stars to the portrait that seem to us as if they were just born from the darkness. He does this for hours until the night sky is set right and as it should be.

When he is finished, he stands and gives the shade a slight tug and guides it as it quietly lifts upward to expose the light of morning. He then lies down in his huge bed to sleep for just a few hours until it is time for him to repeat his eternal ritual: to lower the shade and do his artist's work once again.

Summer Snow

Sitting in the shade, taking a break from cutting the grass, I imagined myself inside of the small snow globe that sits on the coffee table in the living room.

I can picture myself walking out from the little house under the curved glass and looking upward from the short sidewalk.

I can see my wife coming over and picking it up. She gives it a little shake as I hold on tightly to the tiny red gaslight lamppost in the front yard.

Snow begins falling all around. I just stand there breathing in the crisp cold air. A beautiful winter wonderland to enjoy on such an abnormally hot day.

Then I tell myself it's time to get back to work as I shake the snow from my boots and head back toward the mower.

Horse Pills

It began late in the evening and started with me tossing my cookies, although I don't remember the last time I actually ate a cookie.

That progressed into coughing my brains out, but obviously, I still have some gray matter intact or I would be incapable of writing this.

As the evening went on, I started burning up with fever but up to that point I had not been turned to ash and blown away by the ceiling fan to scatter into all corners of the room.

Next, I began to sweat my ass off, but in fact, it was still attached to my posterior supported, I suppose, on the other side by my belly button.

I was given a dose of so-called horse pills which could be easily swallowed by a pony much less a full-grown horse. I began to feel better after taking them.

The next day my appetite returned, and I started to eat like a horse, whose pills worked wonders, and perhaps that is why they are called what they are called, and their size doesn't really matter at all.

The Fate of Words

On this bright and early Sunday morning, we are having a pre-buffet Bloody Mary. While everyone else is milling about enjoying their beverages, with a choice of pickled okra, spicy green beans or boiled shrimp as garnishes, I have quietly escaped for a bit to my little writing area accompanied by my thoughts.

Thoughts that I now squeeze through a pencil all concentrated into the tip of this one sharp point. Those thoughts are now etched deeply into the paper, each letter a few grains of lead that have come together onto the page. Letters written in cursive as if holding hands to form words. The words attach themselves to the page and stay there until peeled away by the reader, just like you. Only the top layer, of course. A copy of each word is made in the mind of the reader. That's how I hope for it to work.

Then somewhere along the way, I write something that makes no sense to me after I read it back to myself. Naturally, I don't want you, the reader, to have an impression in your mind that is incoherent, so I turn the pencil around to completely erase the words. Those words are now inside tiny curled bits of rubber and are swept off the paper with the back of my hand. Those words will eventually become stuck to the bottom of shoes worn by those walking in and out of my small writing room, undoubtedly coming by to check on me and refill my empty drink glass.

From there, they will be taken on walks back throughout the house. Eventually, they will be trampled upon enough for the rubber to disintegrate and leave the words just dangling in the air, thoroughly mixed together like the cocktails, words from an incomprehensible phrase waiting for an opportunity to be used again by me. Waiting for that moment when I have had one too many drinks and blurt out something totally unintelligible, shake my head and think to myself, "Where the hell did that come from?"

Speed Bump

I prefer my watch to be rectangular or square at the very least. A round watch is a timepiece where the hands of time just continue to go spinning around in a circle, seemingly endless boring circles of consistency.

A rectangular watch somehow makes me feel that for a few times every hour, it is obligatory that time hit a speed bump. It gets caught up in that awkward adjustment that it is required to make at every corner, somehow slowing it down. I like to think that there is an obstacle every so often that gets in time's way, makes it miss a step. And right now, anything to persuade it to slow down would be helpful.

Of course, eventually someone will notice and point out to me that my watch is running slow. I always just smile, say "thank you," and reset it. I don't mind having to reset my watch on those occasions because I'm certain that it isn't really running slow; it's just me getting a few more seconds of precious time in my life than anyone who wears a circular watch.

Eight to Five

I never really had an eight-to-five job like most people. I always wondered how folks who worked those hours for five or six days a week ever got anything else done. There are so many trivial things that everyone must manage from day to day. With that said, I have, over time, perfected my own methodology. The way life works for me today is that I spend most of my time gazing out the window or reading poetry for inspiration. It's what I do, and it consumes every hour of my workday, but I still manage to get what I consider the other less important things done anyway. It has become a perfectly normal process for me. On the plus side, I am fortunate enough to have the gracious assistance of others.

When I get ready for bed, I dress appropriately: shirt, pants, socks and shoes. As you would probably guess, trying to get a full night's rest is difficult when you sleepwalk every evening, so I try to make the most of it that I can. During my slumber I get up and have an early morning stroll which is good because I need the exercise. Every morning, I stop in at the local convenience store and purchase a newspaper. To their credit, they don't even try to wake me up anymore. My next stop is the nearby supermarket. Here a cart is placed in front of me by the kind people who work up front that thankfully are used to me by now. They bag my doughnuts and milk then lead me out the front door. Normally I head home from there and my wife kindly brings me to my bed and tucks me under the covers till morning comes.

When I do wake up, I do my work. I think of things to write about. I use that time to look through books and magazines. I pace the floor waiting for something to pop into my head that I deem interesting enough to put to paper. I get the really important things done during those hours. It's what I have been doing all morning today and have continued to do up to this point in the day. It is now time for me to get some of the less important things accomplished. My plan for the afternoon is to take a nap during which time I will cut the lawn. That way it will look pristine for my wife's meeting of her garden club tomorrow. While that meeting is taking place will also be the appropriate time for another nap so I can take care of something trivial like washing the car.

Always Pay Attention to the Details

On a ship at sea, I jumped into the rolling blue ocean from the rail. It was a long way down before I felt the water was warm and tasted saltier than I ever remembered. I splashed about and watched the ship move beyond my sight and over the dark horizon. It was only a few minutes later that I found myself sitting on the edge of the bed, back in my room.

This was the little game I started playing over time. I could do this because something unusual, and as far as I could tell, had happened only to me and no one else aboard. It occurred without any prior notice during my first cruise on this ship, a sort of "out of the blue" moment. When the ship crossed the international date line on our journey, for me, it was yesterday again. First time, every time.

If I was eating dinner at that moment, I was instantly brought back to whatever I was doing yesterday at that very second. If I was standing on the bow being sprayed by the crashing waves out front, I would be transported to the bar, the casino, or wherever I was yesterday at that precise juncture in time. It happened only once each cruise, on the second day, when we crossed the line. It happened every single trip, and no one else noticed any difference. No one knew but me. It was my own personal secret little trick. Maybe it was because my head had been filled with silly thoughts about this circumstance throughout my entire life. Cross the date line, and it's yesterday again. As if nothing had happened. A do-over that I alone take part in every single time on this ship.

On the second night of my first cruise, after having had entirely too much to drink, I fell over the side. At first of course, I panicked. But to my surprise, after the ship crossed the date line, I found myself back in my stateroom in my bed, dry as a bone. That was the beginning of my grand adventures over the side. Over the years, I have done it several times just for the fun of it. Every time we have taken a cruise on this ship, I have taken a late-night dip in the ocean.

Unfortunately, tonight was different. I pushed my little secret too far. I never paid attention to the details. I had never really noticed the direction. I never realized that the ship was always going west to east when I had my fun. My mistake. I should have considered that this time, when we left on the same ship but from a different port, things could change. Tonight, it went east to west.

Now I am here, bobbing like a tiny cork in the ocean after watching the ship sail away in quite the opposite direction from what I was used to. It has been many hours since I lost sight of the ship. I had forgotten that you can cross the date line in the other direction. It's always in the details. And I suppose that for them, those still aboard, it means an entire day will seem to pass before anyone even notices that I am gone.

Prodigy

He remembered, coming in to escape the other children who were outside playing their childish games and then positioned himself where he loved to be, standing there before the empty canvas along with his childhood imagination, he picked up the brush and made a long and wide stroke across its stark white surface with black paint, which he did until it reached the edge where he then continued to paint the air itself, making a thin dark ribbon that went down to the floor, painting a line that then entered the chute at the bottom of a bubble gum machine that happened to be lying on the floor, where he lifted the flap and a robin's egg blue gumball tumbled out past his hand and moved like a miniature bowling ball, rolling along the ribbon of paint and striking the toy ten pins that shattered into pieces from which thousands of slivers each took the form of tiny dark birds that pulled the ribbon of paint up from behind and to the other side of the canvas where they landed in the paint itself and begin to make tiny claw prints on the surface then proceeded to walk about everywhere until the canvas was covered completely to solid black, where the four corners of the painting quickly folded in toward the center and the whole picture swallowed itself and him along with it, which then began to slightly twist and made him feel as if he were riding along the bottom of the spiraling tube, like he was inside a waterslide of flowing whiskey that emptied into a glass sitting on a table outside in the backyard, only to be knocked over by the backhand of unrequited love, the glass spilling its contents out onto the ground where he melted along with the ice cubes and evaporated toward the sky to become part of a cloud that was blown thousands of miles north, where he was then captured inside a drop of water that fell back down to earth as a snowflake and landed on the tongue of a child, who was hit and was hurt during the snowball fight and then was cried out of that child's eye as a tear that slid down the boy's cheek and landed in the snow where it was formed as part of another snowball that hit the outcast child again, and part of that snowball was carried into the schoolhouse on his jacket that he hung up, before he picked up a paintbrush and painted a long dark line across the canvas as all of the other children came in and laughed about his little work of art because they couldn't grasp the depth and intricate complexity of one long dark paint stroke across the stark white canvas, he remembered.

Sounds of the Sea

I was walking through the ruins of a small shop that used to stand here on the beach. It has been many months since the hurricane devastated this place. As I looked around in the debris, I found a perfectly intact nautilus shell. All the others were either cracked or completely destroyed, but for some reason, this one had been spared.

The shop was once a place to buy souvenirs and trinkets which I suppose included the shell I had in my hand. This one was very large, very unique, and it was naturally hard to resist holding it up to my ear to "hear the ocean." That's what everyone has always said: you can hear the splashing of the ocean coming from the opening at the end of the shell.

After caving to my juvenile desire to listen to the sounds of the sea inside, I took the shell with me to the car and set it on the seat across from me. I thought it would make a nice addition to my collection. It wasn't long after I started for home that I began to hear that same swashing sound coming from the shell all the way across the car. It started out very softly then grew louder and louder until I began to also hear the howl of the wind rising to a gale. That's when I looked over at it, and I noticed a tiny stream of water was beginning to flow out of the shell.

In just seconds, that stream became a torrent spewing out of the opening. Saltwater, seaweed and even fish were pouring out of the shell. My car began to fill to the point that I had to open my door to let it run out. When I finally reached my house, I grabbed the nautilus and ran down to the beach where I threw it as far as I could out into the distant waves.

Later that evening as the sun was about to set, maybe it was just my imagination, but I noticed that the tide seemed higher than it should be. Either way, I poured myself a drink and listened to the sounds of the sea. This time while standing on my balcony, far above the beach, just in case.

Best Night's Sleep of Their Lives

I was very tired. It was that restless night's sleep everyone has on occasion. I kept thinking about how I had to get up early, constantly peeking at the light from the clock, wondering if I had set the time for the alarm correctly.

When it went off, I wanted so badly to use the left arrow button, the one that sets the time, to push down on it and run the minutes backward.

To look out the window and see the stars rushing by in the wrong direction. Watch the moon shift through the sky to fall into a lower position. Then, I could turn over and get a few more hours of rest.

No one would be the wiser, and everyone else would wake up in the morning feeling like they had gotten the best night's sleep of their lives.

Nostalgia

I rented an old cottage in a small English town for a few days. A quaint little place on a street with rows of tightly packed stone buildings and chimneys climbing into the sky. I went there with the hope of being inspired. I wanted to write about places that I had studied in pictures from so very long ago. All of them photos from different books about the effects World Wars had on this town and its inhabitants.

It was late, but I popped out for a shandygaff or two and retired after my long journey. When I awoke to take a walk around, this time in the daylight, I stepped through the door, and everything outside, including me, was in black and white. There were times that I thought I had seen myself in some of those old photos but dismissed it as wishful thinking.

Somehow, in that moment, I felt right at home as I began to stroll the lane. Cottages lined the winding street. Some were collapsed with many locals outside stacking bricks and removing rubble. A family was returning to the village with their belongings strapped to both sides of a mule, the older man guiding her slowly along with a stick in his hand.

Outside of one residence was an old woman who was peeling potatoes into a pan on her lap. I stopped to say hello, and we started to talk. She then began to tell me stories of World War Two and what had happened to the town: how some of the people fled and others braved the brutal nights. As I looked around, I could see the repairs were still going on. I thanked her and continued to walk the area and watch the people and view the damage.

I happened upon a small group around the bend where I then rolled up my sleeves and helped them out as best I could. Made a few friends. People were kind enough to share stories and food and drink -- a lot of drink. I returned to my room of color feeling humble and grateful. The sacrifices they made were incredible. I lay on my cot and closed my eyes thinking about those that came before us and what they had endured. I also was thinking how difficult it would be to write about what they had experienced firsthand and that I could only repeat what others told me. It surely wouldn't be the same. It would lack the intensity of living through that experience.

When morning broke, I went out to have another walk, anxious to see the people I met the day before, hoping to share more stories. But this time, everything had changed. The buildings, the people, all quite different from the ones I met yesterday. Their clothing, their seemingly carefree manner. It then came to me that this town looked exactly like some of the much older pictures I had studied. It seemed that I had walked outside and into pre-World War One. Besides their dress and the look of the place, there were other things that helped me reach that conclusion. This time, everything outside, including me, like the older photos, were now in sepia.

I pondered for a moment the strange opportunity I had been given and wondered what I would learn and write about today. That is what was in my thoughts as I turned to watch a squadron of biplanes swoop down from the clouds and begin flying toward us.

Little Man

I sometimes think about that little man inside of me. The one with the wrinkled shirt and rolled up sleeves, top button unbuttoned, his tie pulled down from around his neck. Unshaven and with that cigarette dangling from the side of his mouth, his glasses barely clinging to the tip of his nose.

He spends all his time puttering around the shop doing the things I don't do. He never rests so I can. He tells my hands what to do and my feet where to go. He sits on a nest of thoughts and hatches one when the need arises. He paces back and forth all day trying to come up with something new for me to dream at night.

He plays that projector in my mind as his entertainment while he tells my lungs when to breathe and my heart when it should beat, all the while I am fast asleep. He sets the silent alarm that wakes me every morning; then he rings it for me.

Currently, he is at his desk trying to divide the drops of fluid he possesses into one bottle for tears and another for sweat.

Lately, he seems to be growing weary of his duties; he may be getting tired. But as far as he is concerned, retirement is out of the question. One day, he will just conclude that it's time for a much-deserved repose and descend into a long, deep and solitary sleep.

Coloring Book (For Dinky)

She was lying on the living room floor in front of me, legs crossed and bent at the knees, demonstrating the full power and versatility of a box of crayons. Erratic scribbles were everywhere with mom all the while trying to teach her to stay inside the lines. In time, she will eventually learn to do just that. To keep to the right, everyone in single file. To be in the precise position at arm's length. To march in a school band in perfect unison. To always stay within the lines.

And it will be many years before she is able to unlearn that. To understand that the river carves its own route. To find that you will see more on the winding path less traveled than on a straight paved road with fences in place to keep you from straying. To learn that music doesn't stay inside of the lines but travels out in all directions.

As I watch her, I am reminded of that child who took great pains to completely color the area outside of the little white seal with the ball balanced on his nose. He would leave the seal and ball exactly as they were and colored a world for them outside of the lines, surrounding them with crayon pictures of the sun and sky and stars.

Weighing In

It had been a while since I stood on a scale, the instrument of my torture. I had been trying to take care of myself as was suggested by my doctor, but I must admit that I was somewhat surprised that a trip to his office for a check-up would reveal that I had lost ten pounds.

I guess I should rephrase that. I suppose I didn't really lose it. It's not as if I forgot it in the back seat of a cab. I didn't lose it in the same sense as it would be if I lost my keys. To be perfectly honest, I'm not sure where it went or how it went where it did, but it's gone.

It does have to go somewhere. It just doesn't disappear into thin air. Maybe it disappears into fat air. Perhaps it dissolves into the atmosphere in tiny microscopic specks and attaches itself to people without their knowledge. If that is the case, my loss is someone else's gain.

And yes, I've been in that position, too. I have been that guy who put both feet on the scale and wondered how I gained ten pounds. I didn't know where it came from, but there it is. I may have walked by someone whose frame, at that precise moment, was losing the weight that was put on to it by a cream filled doughnut and I just happened by while he was jogging it off. It left him and attached itself to me without me being the one who enjoyed that doughnut. Maybe that's how fat redistributes itself. Maybe there is only so much fat in the world, and it is moving from person to person.

So, if you have been eating properly and exercising but stepped foot on that bathroom scale this morning and were flabbergasted that you have gained weight, I do apologize. It could be my fault for losing part of that ten pounds somewhere near you.

On the positive side, you won't be like that person who I read about today, just disappearing one night, never to be heard from again. That, too, may be my fault. I had been so heavy for so long that I felt like I was using more than my fair share of gravity. Maybe so much of it that, perhaps one day, without being noticed by anyone, an unfortunate skinny someone had just floated off into the sky for lack of enough gravity to keep him attached to the earth. He is now just listed as a missing person. If I am even remotely to blame, once again, my apologies.

More Useless Thoughts About Death (A Dark Ride)

A bird outside of the living room window this morning lay dead in the driveway, obviously the victim of one of the neighborhood cats. I buried it in the shade of an oak tree all the while thinking about death himself and what would happen if death himself died. You must admit that we curse death every day, but if he died, nothing else would. I can see it now, death lying in an open casket, wearing his dark robes and his scythe by his side. Next to him, arrangements of flowers that cannot wither and die.

I'm sure I'd give it no thought at first. It would seem like a welcome gift. Death is dead; long live life. But a day after I returned home from a fishing trip and I could still hear the bass jumping around inside of the ice chest, I would give it that second thought. If I cooked them, would they still be flopping around in the pan and then on the plate as I tried to eat them? If death himself should die, every bird not buried under an oak tree would eventually lose their feathers and just become a mesh of flying bones that the wind passes through. Every cat that prowls my yard would be reduced to being moving skeletons with useless claws.

Then it could be me: lying in the hospital writhing in pain with no way to bring it to an end. It would be a welcome relief when the skin fell from my bones, an alleviation for me but not for the others who would continue to suffer.

Eventually, we would join the countless creatures walking the streets forever bumping into each other, all unable to see, and all unable to appreciate the aroma of the endless multitude of flowers that were beginning to blanket the earth.

Yellow Pencils

There was an old joke about whatever happened to the Yellow Pencil #1. I don't recall the joke itself, but I do remember wondering what exactly was wrong with that pencil.

Why consider it a failure and move on to #2? Did it only write backwards? Did it continuously and constantly write upside down? Could it only write numbers? Could it only write in yellow? Did it only let you use it to keep score on a golf card? Did it refuse to write at all?

Maybe it was something as simple as the eraser declined to erase words that started with the letter Y. Or, perhaps it only and solely erased vowels. What was its problem?

Of course, on their second try, they reached perfection -- the Yellow Pencil #2. It performed exactly as advertised every time without a single problem of any kind. One disaster, one perfection.

I had always hoped that the inventors would get back together and create a Yellow Pencil #3. Something that would be a wonderful combination of the #1 and #2. A perfect collaboration of the faulty #1 and the flawless #2. It would be a mastery of ingenuity that if used to write words that are in English, would always and only write those words entirely in French.

Flip Books

I remember those books. A few pages stacked between two cardboard covers. Each page contained an image slightly different than the one that came next. Flipping through it a page at a time gave each book an authentic cinematic animation.

Buster Keaton moving up and down as he sat on the steel rail attached to the driver wheels of an old steam train. Bugs Bunny being chased by Elmer Fudd. Roy Rogers blazing across the plains riding his golden palomino Trigger. A moving picture that could be played out in my hands at any time I chose.

And as a youngster, it brought me great joy to realize that I possessed a piece of a movie, a scene from a cartoon or a portion of my favorite television show. It was a wonderful feeling to know that I could bring them to life whenever I wished. It was special for me to appreciate that I carried in the back pocket of my jeans, an exhibition on how to use nunchakus -- presented by Bruce Lee himself.

I Have Questions About Clowns

What makes someone want to become a clown?

Were they class clowns back in school?

Why are some clown faces sad and others are happy?

Is it the costumes or the makeup or the thought of maybe one day being able to wash in a bucket of confetti?

Is it the appeal of the horns or maybe the flower that waters you?

Why is only one clown in the clown alley fortunate enough to own a car?

Where do they go in it?

Do they go off to clown college, the bastion of knowledge for all things clown?

Do they take classes such as Red Noses 101 or An Introduction to Wigs?

Would you really want to walk a mile in their shoes?

Déjà Vu

I am baffled this evening by an overwhelming feeling that I am having. I walked into this room and turned on the light at the precise moment that lightning struck outside; the power went off, followed by a siren screaming down the street.

I'm not sure if it was the lightning or the siren or the sensation that I had done this before that made the hair on the back my neck rise to attention. It seemed like an illusion was being played out on my senses. I felt as though I had been pulled backwards, fell, and became immersed in an experience that I had in the past while also succeeding to drag the present back with me.

But that's not the whole story. What makes it especially odd is that I feel like I've had this Déjà Vu before. Like I had the same Déjà Vu more than once -- the exact same one. If so, I know that somewhere in a stack of notebooks I have kept over the years, I must have written it down just as I am doing now because that is what I do. And if it is really the second time I have had this same one, it also means that I would have written down the description of this event at least once before today.

I gave some thought to going back and checking to be sure, but I'm afraid that if I couldn't find any evidence, if what I'm writing at this moment is my only proof, I would always wonder to myself if any of it ever really happened at all, even once.

No Stone Left Unturned

I lost a button. It was one of those milky white colored ones that are often placed on ordinary white dress shirts. I wasn't certain where it decided to leap off after untying itself from the edge of the cloth, but as it happened before I got home, I do know it was not in the house.

I began my search outside. I started with the small pebbles in the front garden. I turned them all over one by one and found absolutely nothing. From there I progressed to the street in front of the house, and then I moved on to the stones in my neighbors' yards.

I turned over every stone I could find, but still there was nothing. I went on for miles down the road until I eventually found myself turning over every stone in the entire city. Some people seemed a bit upset as you might understand, but I had to do what I had to do because I still hadn't found my button.

Continuing my complete and absolutely thorough search, I went from state to state, and I would not be deterred by the fact that I had to rent various pieces of heavy equipment to turn over the larger rocks and boulders. Even being forced to hire giant cranes did not slow me down as I pressed on with my quest.

I finally exhausted every possibility after I turned over every stone there was on the entire planet. I did regret having to stop without ever finding that button, but I must say that the pyramids of Giza look quite different upside down with the pointy tops balancing them in the ground.

Language Barrier

While I was in Italy, I watched as a young lady in her finest ski wear yelled into a crevice at the edge of the Italian Alps. The response from the mountains was a sweet, "Ciao."

When I was on the Swiss side of the mountains, an older gentleman bellowed out and it came back to him as a hardy, "Hallo."

The next day, I stood by while a sweet child squeaked out her cry in the French part of the mountains and was rewarded with a gentle, "Bonjour."

Now I don't speak any of those languages, and that has caused many problems throughout my journey.

But it was refreshing to note that when I yelled, "Hello," into any of those mountains, none of them held it against me, and they were all courteous enough to respond in English.

A Better Place

There used to be this plain jane little jar I remember from when I was a kid. My grandmother had it sitting on her bureau. The letters on the side of the container said it was called vanishing cream. When I asked, I was told that it was supposed to make your blemishes disappear as a foundation or something like that.

I was a child back then, so I naturally compared it in my young mind with the jar of vanishing cream I used to see in the *Tom and Jerry* cartoons. In their case, it wasn't makeup but instead, made anything that it touched disappear. Jerry would steal it, slather it all over himself, and then hilarity would ensue.

I would like to find a jar of that cream -- the cartoon variety. There are so many things that I would like to make go away. So many bad things. Even as a kid, the world seemed like it could sometimes be a horrible place. There were instances that I imagined I'd rub it all over myself and just disappear to somewhere else.

I am not sure of exactly where I hoped it would take me, but I just wanted it to be a better place. A place like the cartoon world, where no matter how bad they were hit, there was never any pain. They would just shrug it all off and go back to the unfolding story unscathed. Never any injuries. Just more cartoon fun.

We never actually saw my grandmother use that cream, but we, the kids, often wondered about it. My grandmother seemed to always know when we were up to something. Being the children that we were, we believed that she would rub it on, disappear just like in the cartoons, and spy on us from a better place.

Not soon after, she got very sick and was in a lot of pain. One day, I went to visit. They told me she died and went to a better place. I was a kid. I just assumed she got tired of the pain, used the cream and vanished to the somewhere else I often wondered about -- somewhere that pain could not reach her anymore.

I sit here now, as an adult, flipping through the channels and occasionally find myself stopping when I come to an old *Tom and Jerry* cartoon, hoping to see an episode where Jerry steals vanishing cream from his cartoon grandmother who only uses it to spy on his and Tom's hijinks, all done from a better place.

Guest Bathroom

When I was in little school (that's what they called the first three grades at the time), we used to write on something called manila paper. It wasn't like the paper of today. It was a bit coarse, and you could almost see the grain from the tree. It had thin blue horizontal lines to help us keep our place when we were practicing writing letters. If we made an error, we would easily erase that fragile paper sometimes to the extent of rubbing a hole through the paper itself. That small letter z or the capital A, the one we so painstakingly penciled in with childlike precision just disappeared along with the paper.

That's what I was reminded of when I went to do some cleaning in the bathroom of what was then, our new house. I chose a product that was simply described as a deep cleaning spray. Unfortunately, I didn't know how deep. After the fact, I did recall and consider that, yes, I was always the child who was guilty of erasing a paper until I wore a hole through it, but in hindsight, maybe it wasn't just me.

When I used this spray on the bathroom mirror, it worked just as advertised. It went very very deep. So deep in fact, that it completely wiped away my reflection. In my bewilderment I wasn't sure if my image was now somewhere on the cloth, or if I had managed to once again do what I did as a kid -- just in a different way. Like, maybe, I erased a hole in the mirror and my face went with it.

Perhaps someday, I will figure it out, but as of now, I don't use that bathroom. I pretty much avoid it all together. Everyone else's reflection shows up in there perfectly fine, just not mine. It's as if I wrote the letters BOB on a mirror of manila and rubbed it until I rubbed a hole through the letters once again. So, to make things easier on myself, especially when shaving, that particular place in the house is now referred to as the guest bathroom.

Sing for Your Supper

Until today, I had not heard the term used in quite a long time. In case you don't know, it refers to those that used to travel from town to town, balladeers meandering through Europe, singing songs and telling tales for food and drink. I could never have been such a person. I have been told that my voice is comparable to the movement of a rusty old hinge.

So, when I try to imagine myself as a minstrel in that century, and my only means of being fed would rely on singing, I can only picture myself sitting at the end of a long wooden table, a thin and exceedingly gaunt man with a tight grip on a fork in one hand and a knife in the other, with both of those utensils showing the beginning signs of rust.

Portrait of Bluegills

I walked into the spare bedroom and noticed that the painting of fish on the wall was askew. It was tilted to one side. Now the fish looked as though they were swimming downward. They were meant to appear a certain way, to be swimming straight across the painting.

I imagine if I left it that way, the background would slowly begin to turn darker. The deeper they would swim into the lake the less light would shine through. Soon, they wouldn't be able to see anything, and I would not be able to see them. That just wouldn't do. So, I straightened it up before things got out of hand. I fancied for a second that one of the bluegills, who normally stares wide-eyed and directly ahead as he should, winked at me in appreciation.

And what if the painting had tilted the other way? Would they have swam up to the surface and then out of the lake entirely? Would I enter the room one day and see the painter of the picture actually in the picture, looking upward toward the fish that were ascending ever so slowly into the sky? A few days later I could come into the room and all I would see on the canvas was that the fish had disappeared into the darkness of deep space.

I wasn't going to take that chance, and that's why I perfectly leveled it out. After all, I didn't buy a painting of the murky depths of a lake, nor did I buy one depicting outer space. I just want to see the painting as it was intended -- fish endlessly swimming but going nowhere.

Bookmark

Normally, I will use anything as a bookmark, whatever is handy. A coupon ripped from the morning paper or a subscription card that fell from a magazine. Today would be different.

As I was rifling through my left desktop drawer, I came across an actual bookmark. It was labeled as a Blooming Expression Card. A bookmark with an adornment on one end of pressed paper that was in the shape of a butterfly and sprinkled within its wings were a few dried seeds of wildflowers.

There was also a date on this card that told me the seeds that it held were pressed over ten years ago. The user is supposed to cut along the dotted line and plant the paper butterfly with the promise of wildflowers blooming.

I decided to use it exclusively, and for the next few winter months, it became my normal place holder. From book to book and beyond, it found its position between stories of all kinds.

In the spring, I decided to do as instructed and cut along the dotted line. I was happy to plant them for these seeds had been silent for long enough. They had waited patiently for years and now have spent the winter absorbing the stories and words of every page where they were asked to save a place.

It is I that am now patiently waiting, waiting for them to bloom. I'm sure that as the flowers grow, they will be visited by bees with whom a floret will share a story it holds. Each will tell a tale, all delivered in small portions just as they were taken in. I'm certain, too, that the bees will return every day to hear a different part of a story conveyed to them by a different and colorful wildflower.

Animal Crackers

For as long as I can remember, Animal Crackers have been housed in little yellow and red boxes, divided into sections and of course, appear behind bars. Tasty little cookie treats that I grew up with along with everyone else.

But in the society of today, it is frowned upon to have animals in cages, even ones that are cookies. Somehow there was an intervention of sorts, and they have now been freed. No longer are the little wafers of goodness being held captive. The bars have been removed from the boxes allowing the creatures unbound freedom.

So, it was no surprise when the store manager dropped his cup of coffee, and the patrons at the registers stared with their collective mouths agape as the animals, one by one, began leaving their boxes.

A single gorilla made his way over to the fruit section using his short muscular looking arms to swing his way upward toward the bananas. An elephant was trying her best, using her tiny trunk in an attempt to open a can of unsalted peanuts.

A polar bear was standing on his hind legs but was still not able to reach the bottom of the meat freezer door.

A miniature lion was tearing into a scrap of roast beef that was laying on the floor behind the deli counter.

As for the rest, they all made a hasty exit out into the parking lot where they gathered together in a large group after departing the store. Many more were reported to be leaving stores across the city and state.

As I stood there eating my cookie, I could see in the distance what appeared to be many millions of angry Animal Crackers crowding the streets, all headed in this direction.

Aquarium

For some time now, I have been a landlord but not in the conventional sense that would normally come to one's mind. I am, in fact, the owner and sole proprietor of a twenty-gallon freshwater aquarium.

My tenants do not pay me in money but reward me by bringing the gift of calmness to the room. They stare out at me every day, and at times, look as though they would appreciate having a sit-down with the keeper of the tank.

I have often wished that I was small enough to make a dive inside. To hold my nose then jump in from the plastic rim at the top of the front glass and don that scuba suit that is perpetually floating in there.

I'm sure I'd be safe considering there seems to be an adequate amount of air that is being supplied. There is always a constant trail of bubbles that go unused streaming to the surface.

I would go down to my lodgers and listen to their complaints. They could tell me if they weren't happy with the food, maybe inform me that the water is too cold.

They might want to know why it is presumed that the guppies will live in that small cave while the goldfish get to reside in a castle. All of them would want me to get rid of that eyesore, the skeleton sitting on the toilet.

Overall, I believe it would be an interesting experience. And before I returned to the surface to climb out, I would have to see what, if anything, is hidden in that treasure chest.

Signs

A friend said to me that she was thinking about her husband who had left us all behind a week earlier, when a small red mosquito hawk appeared on her windowsill. She took it as a sign from him, that he was around in some way, temporarily slipping from the ether to come back and watch her that day.

I read a story in the newspaper about a woman who asked her mom, shortly before she passed, to give her a sign when she got to heaven. On the day her mother died, a wild cardinal came to her and stayed with her for hours before winging away and disappearing into the evening sky.

Some ancients believed that people come back, momentarily possessing these animals and looking at us through their eyes, trying to give us a sign. That's why, when I gaze into the eyes of any creature large or small, I can't help but wonder if a loved one long gone is in there looking back at me from the other side.

Video

A commercial for the app on my cell phone said that my video would "Be alive in there!" That the visual images would seem so realistic, it would appear as if they were indeed living in my phone.

Apparently, the recording I took of us yesterday at the lake, now has a life of its own. I watched it when we got home last night. I must admit, the look on your face, the way the sun filtered through your hair, it was truly lifelike.

But I do know me, and if there were a tiny me living in there, I'm sure I am bored duplicating the same situation over and over. If a replica of me were alive inside the phone, I've probably decided to do what I wanted to do in there.

After it was viewed several times, maybe the me in there grew tired of the repetition and determined that we had gone elsewhere yesterday. It's possible that if I turned on that video right now, I never made it to the lake and neither did you. We both went to a carnival instead to enjoy the Ferris wheel and laugh over some sticky cotton candy.

The video from yesterday would now only contain an empty lake with a rowboat tied to the dock, still moving up and down from the current made by the wind.

I'm sure the other version of me that exists in the phone made a video of our day at the funfair and that I could play it back right now to find out if we had a good time.

Palms of Proserpine

I spent a great afternoon sitting out on this balcony, here in the lovely city of Proserpine. Nothing like relaxing while having a drink and watching the runners, walkers, and bicyclers that are using the path below to take a break in the shade of the palms.

It was then that those large and full palms began encouraging my customary notion to conjure up fanciful ways for normal things to happen. At that moment, the outline of the palms on the ground were clearly defined by the intense sunlight.

I had noticed that occasionally a bit of cloud cover would cause them to slightly blur around the edges. Showing us their infinite patience, that was not the instance the palms were looking for. They seemed to wait for the other moments, when very dark clouds would make the shadows disappear completely.
I believe that this is the time, the time that the palms collected the shade produced by those black clouds and stored it inside of themselves.

There it remains until once again the palms are asked to help give comfort to the many. Delivering a respite for the weary in need of a bit of shade from the sun and something for me to muse about this beautiful afternoon.

Happier

Right now, I am happier. Happier than I was last year when I had to get that root canal, and certainly happier than a few months later when I was bent over in pain from that kidney stone.

Happier than last month when my beloved Mr. Big had to be put down or the week after that when the cat got out and I haven't seen her since.

As I look up at the partially starry sky tonight, I am happier than I was an hour ago when the car broke down on the side of the interstate -- miles from nowhere.

Happier than I was a few minutes later when I realized that the battery in my phone was dead.

Happier still than when I understood I would have to walk by the side of the highway in the moonless dark of night to find some help.

Happier than I was just a second ago, before it started to rain.

Trouble with Elevators

People think I am afraid of elevators. I suppose that may be somewhat true, but only to a small degree, and not for the reasons they want to believe. They think I have a phobia about riding in them. That is completely untrue. I just got tired of trying to explain it a long time ago, and besides, no one believes me.

You see, the problem started one day when I got into an elevator in the Marriot Hotel on Canal Street in New Orleans, and when I got out, I was in the lobby of The Ritz Carlton Hotel a few blocks away. In the beginning, that was something I could handle. I could just walk back. But later, it got much worse.

One day I walked into an elevator in Atlanta and walked out of one in San Francisco. That, ultimately, was a six-hundred-dollar elevator ride. Sometime after that, I got into an elevator in New York and got out in New Zealand. I'm sure you can guess that it was an extremely expensive plane ticket -- not to mention my lack of luggage, personal toiletries, and the whole passport thing.

The final straw for me was when I walked into an elevator in the year 2010, and when the doors opened, I saw my mother standing there holding the hand of a small boy that happened to be me. She was so young, and so was I, maybe three or four. "We" were apparently standing outside of the doors waiting for the elevator that was going up while "I" was going down. It was probably the year 1956 or 1957, as close as I can guess. They didn't recognize me, of course, as I was a grown man, and naturally, I didn't get out.

When the elevator doors opened on the bottom floor, I had fortunately gone back in time only two days. I say "fortunately" because the day before this unusual elevator ride, I had cut myself slicing onions, and it required several stitches. I avoided that accident by getting take-out the second time around.

So, yes, I do not ride elevators. And it's not because of a phobia, or I'm afraid of confined spaces, or anything remotely like that. I don't ride elevators because I don't want to get into one today and accidentally walk out into 1936. I don't believe there is a plane ticket for that.

Creative Juices

We have all heard the expression, "My creative juices were flowing." As far as I am personally concerned, I don't know if I would characterize it so much as juices as I would a pool of thought, one that just sits there very still and placid.

That's how the pool usually is during the day. Most of the time, I find myself standing at a distance and throwing rocks at the edge of the barrier that holds the pool in place, hoping to break open a crack to let the thoughts flow out.

But once again, in my case, creative juices always seem to begin flowing in the middle of the night. And it's not so much a real flow, but instead, it is a slow drip into my dreams that always wakes me at one or two in the morning.

Why can't they be a quiet pool, settled in my mind for eight hours, resting there without a ripple until dawn? Instead, they begin as a drib and eventually flow out like a faucet wide open, one that I spill out onto the page in the darkness of night.

Soon, the ink of ideas runs out and drains the pool until it is empty. After that, the dripping stops, and I can go back to sleep while it fills itself again. I really do wish that every so often it would happen at a decent hour.

Until then, I suppose I should not complain. It's much better than the pool drying up all together, my mind then becoming parched with thirst for lack of any creative juices flowing . . . or trickling . . . or just dripping.

Blinded by the Light

My mind's eye always conjures up only one version of the past. It always sees things the same. There may be some slight variations that will occur, such as the hour of day, the color of the flowers on the table, that sort of thing. But for the most part, the images are rooted in there very deep. Other than those subtleties, it always plays things back the way I believe that I saw them.

But is it the actual version of what happened, or did my mind change an angle or two over time? Does my mind reshape the truth to make it a more comfortable fit inside of my memory? Does it round off the edges so they aren't as sharp when brushed by my passing a recollection? Does it make changes that if brought out into the light of truth, my mind's eye would be blinded by the reflection?

Cheat

A man reading a book is a man in two worlds. One part tethered to the chair of reality while another part of him has escaped to the inside of the book, walking the trails of the story. The sentences he follows lead him down a perfectly paved sidewalk all the while talking to him as they take him deeper toward the heart of the story.

But sometimes, he becomes so sure of himself that he ignores much of what they have to say and tries to speed recklessly ahead. Of course, he's positive he knows the direction. "This is how I would have written it," he says to himself. "I knew this was going to happen," he thinks as he strolls across and over to the top of the next page, only to be confronted by a group of words huddled together in front of him, blocking his way.

They were something that he didn't expect to see. And when that crowd of words begins to attempt to push him to go in another direction, he becomes confused. He then finds himself lost because he was so certain of where the trail would steer him, positive he couldn't be fooled by a few words trying to mislead him.

It is at this juncture that the man sitting in the chair and holding the book, pulls himself out of the story. He then quickly scans the room to see if anyone is watching and sneaks a peek at the last page.

Levels of Heaven

Someone was feeding our cat while we were away for a week and left the empty cans in the kitchen garbage can. When we came into the house, my wife said that it stunk to high heaven. While taking out the offending bag, I thought about her remark.

That expression has been around forever so it should be a given that if there is a high heaven, there must be other levels. It seems that the person who coined the phrase must have had some insight and knew that somewhere along the way, heaven became separated by society.

That poses many questions in my mind. *Do the angels in high heaven wear finery that includes twenty-four carat gold halos? Do the angels in the bottom of heaven float on street corner clouds and beg for wings?*

I would guess that most angels are in middle heaven, just your average angel. They probably all have jobs as guardians or tapping people on the shoulder when they are trying to make a difficult decision. And what are the jobs available in lower heaven like?

Do the angels in high heaven have anything to do but sit at home and give orders to the servants that come up to work from lower heaven? Do they scurry about getting themselves ready for the big party while periodically checking to make certain the angels in their employ are doing a proper job polishing their expensive halos and perfectly ironing the pleats into their long white robes?

Do the angels from lower heaven have to get down on hands and knees while they scrub and shine the vast dance floor for the festivities, the immense and legendary head of a pin?

Shopping

I have never seen a woman, or anyone else for that matter, that can disappear into a department store faster than she can. I blink; and she's gone. It's as if she dissolved into the air taking the form of a spirit. I know she is in here. I can see racks of dresses move by themselves as if a discerning hand has swept over them as it went by.

I know she just walked through a spray of perfume because before it could dissipate, I saw the mist from the Oscar that she atomized lingering in the air. It still has a hole through it that is in the exact shape of her body. Shoes walk on their own ambling over to a spot where they attempt to match themselves with purses.

At that point, I know it is time to go out to the chair that is always by the front door and take a seat because I also know that it won't be long before she reappears out of a haze directly in front of me. She will be surrounded by a swirling cloud of smoke that just materializes, and then she will step out from what appears to be a portal she discovered in a dressing room on the other side of the store that is closed behind her.

And as always, she will have no bags because everything she tried on looked hideous.

Strings

We have had a string of perfect weather. Each day is like a small bright knot on that string, one I like to imagine that I could pass across my fingertips to remember every individual day in that string.

And today is no exception. But with the onset of rain in the future that will bring this sunny string to an end, I made the decision to hang on to a different kind of string and go parasailing this afternoon.

While on my journey pretending to be a balloon bouncing on a string, I saw ahead of me a rainbow arcing across the sky. As I was pulled faster and closer to it, my body instinctively contorted itself into a ball.

At the last second, I opened my eyes only to witness the mass of my torso crashing into it. I tried to swing around, and as I did, I saw the impact had broken it up, and I watched the splintered colors falling into the sea.

When my ride was over, and I was back on land, I noticed that some of the smaller pieces of the rainbow had stuck to my shirt, and some of them had even found their way inside the waistband of my bathing suit.

One by one, I picked them off and out and then rolled them up in my fingers into tiny balls. Since the weatherman was calling for a string of bad weather to pass through, I placed the colorful balls in a small bowl by my front door.

When this string of rain comes to an end, I will create another string. I will go outside, bowl in hand, and one after another, hurl my rainbow remnants back up into the sunny sky and see if it's possible to create a string of rainbows.

Empty Dreams

I was having an otherwise uneventful dream when some of the characters in the dream decided to leave. I had no control over their actions because I was asleep, and you know how dreams can be.

They escaped through pores in my scalp and slid down the hairs on my head, using them like slippery curved poles to reach my pillow. From there, they descended rapidly down the sheets, then dashed off across the floor and out of the room. The tiny little inhabitants that would normally be in my dream were scampering around my house and probably getting into everything.

The rest of the characters in my dream, who were thrown off by the new but ultimately humdrum scenario, decided to follow them. The room in my dream was now empty. And since I was asleep, I could only dream the rest of the night of a vacant room. At first, I wasn't sure where they went after they left my dream until my neighbor and I were having a discussion the next day. He told me about this strange dream he had and that he had no idea who some of the people in his dream were.

He said that most of those that occupied this dream were the usual ones, that for some reason, always seem to be there every night in every dream he has. They included the magician and the piano player along with a blackjack dealer and a lion tamer.

As he began to describe the new people to me, I quickly realized they were my characters, the ones that deserted me in my sleep. They had gone out to find another dream because apparently mine was too boring.

Tonight, I hope they return and bring with them some of the seemingly fascinating participants from my neighbor's dreams. It sounds like it would be an entertaining dream for both my characters and I to have. And unfortunately for my neighbor, he would, of course, fall off to sleep and dream the entire night about an empty room and wonder why.

Just a Normal Day for a Finch

I saw a finch today with vivid red and yellow plumage poised at the end of a narrow branch right outside of the window of the hospital. He wasn't doing anything particularly unusual, just being a finch as always.

I couldn't help but notice that he had slight streaks of cobalt blue in his feathers, an added touch of grace and beauty that brought me joy to see on a morning that was otherwise filled with anything but.

I reflected for a moment about how many others in the course of the day would see this same resplendent tiny bird and feel as I do now. How many times in the average day of a finch does it share its loveliness with someone who might need a lift of the spirit? How many besides myself will be awe inspired by its merely being there?

I felt as though he was a message for us, as is any work of nature, a colorful note passed to us that is quietly stating the simple beauty that is life. A small reminder of the things we rarely see and appreciate that are normally right in front of us.

And what strikes me as the most poignantly innocent part of all is that it will never know how much happiness it brings by just being itself, just a normal day for a finch.

Procrastination

I stood looking through the front window to see the bright and beautiful day outside. The sun was bathing the palm trees and the flowers in a nourishing light. The postman smiled and waved when he went by as did the neighbor walking his terrier. I thought to myself that it would be the perfect day to get some work done around the house, even though I really didn't feel like it. But after giving it some thought, I couldn't think of anything that absolutely needed to be done on this gorgeous day, nothing that couldn't wait until tomorrow.

And since I could already see what today was like outside of my window, I became curious about what tomorrow would bring. I reached up to the top right and left corners of the window and started to pull them back. I peeled away the window of today, along with its superb view, then set it aside after I rolled it up into a long tube which I leaned against the wall. What I then saw outside was a torrential rainstorm being driven sideways towards the house by a fierce wind. The postman was having to maneuver his way around huge puddles while being splashed by cars going by. The neighbor and his dog were nowhere to be seen.

Once I found out what I needed to know, I put today's window back in place. I unrolled it over tomorrow's view and began to once again appreciate today's scenery while contemplating what little chore I should accomplish before tomorrow's deluge. It was then that I noticed a small puddle forming on the floor. I apparently didn't seal one of the corners fully, and some of tomorrows rain was dripping in and down the sill.

After I made sure that corner was completely secured, I went outside to inspect the other side of the window. I saw a small crack in the caulking that I hadn't noticed before. This was something that couldn't wait. I surely wouldn't be able to do it tomorrow, so I went out and fixed the little area around the window where the water was going to be coming in the next day. That way, I got a chore done, and I also wouldn't have to deal with cleaning up the water again tomorrow. I guess the old saying is true. Never put off till tomorrow what you can do today.

Dinner Reservation

I was visiting the grave of a dear friend on what had turned out to be a most lovely Sunday afternoon. While walking back to my little blue rental car, I saw a grave site that made me feel the need to stop for a time and examine the possibilities that must go through the mind of a Mr. John Meyers.

At my feet was a plot that contained two places side by side but with only a single headstone. Chiseled into the reddish-brown granite was the following information. Cherry Meyers, Born August 17, 1939, Died May 19, 2007. Below that was the name John Meyers, Born December 31, 1937, Died . . . and the rest was blank.

I began to think about Mr. Meyers coming out here and what he must think, as I know I would. I'm certain that he makes frequent visits to his wife as any caring husband would. I know that to be true because it's spelled out here on the headstone: Loving Husband.

But it occurs to me that every time he comes, he must always look at that incomplete date with some normal and expected uneasiness. That after a few years, his visits would be met with some apprehension. Probably because he has this overwhelming fear that one day he may come for a visit and he will be greeted by a small man that sits waiting on a chair next to the grave, smiling and holding a hammer and chisel in his hands. That every time he makes the journey to the top of this hill, it is etched in his mind (no pun intended) that no matter what way it will eventually happen to him; he will end up here.

If he were to die in a train wreck in France or be the victim of a sky diving experience gone wrong in Bolivia, this is where they would bring him. As for myself, I'm not sure I would like to carry those thoughts around in my head for the rest of my life. I suppose that's because it would make me feel as though I had a dinner reservation at God's table, and that I am only waiting for the invitation to be delivered so I can be sure of the exact date that I am supposed to show up.

That's How It Works

It all started with the apple I certainly didn't eat, but that didn't matter. I still managed to carry the burden of original sin around with me. That's what they called it in Catholic school. It wasn't until I was baptized that it was cleansed from my soul. Original sin was washed from me or from anyone else who gets baptized simply by being dunked in a pool. That's the way it works.

From there, we pretty much all transgressed that blessing and dirtied our souls with other sins that we then confessed to a man behind a thin-veiled screen inside of a tiny room. A few prayers of penance later, our souls were once again pristine. And that's how it worked, and continued to work, for a very long time.

These days, I prefer a different method. I take my soul out and fold it neatly on the table where it sits until I also gather up the dirty bath towels and bedsheets. One load of clothes for the laundry. Of course, I clean them with an environmentally friendly detergent. And there they go, out with all of the other dirt in the rinse water. Out through the pipes and into a stream and then a river, where my sins are floating around with the other silent debris. That's how it works.

I then restore my soul inside of me all fresh and with the scent of lilac dryer sheets. My sins may eventually find their way into a tributary that feeds the pipes of a local brewery. They will go unseen and certainly evade all filters. From there, they might find themselves fermented, poured inside of a bottle, and distributed to a local pub. One evening in the future, some unsuspecting fellow that is normally good natured, will down that beer and suddenly feel the uncontrollable need to punch the stranger standing next to him. That's how it works.

Resolution

As I lie here in the dark and stillness of the bedroom, I can hear the soft chatter coming from the kitchen counter. It is my own fault. I set them there, right next to each other. I placed the box of assorted doughnuts I had purchased, and the fresh baked Christmas cookies given to me by a neighbor, side by side. At first, it was just soft banter. Later, it escalated into a loud vocal world of pastry wars.

The cream-filled doughnuts were telling the glazed they would be first. After all, they carried the gift, the prize of cream that could not be offered by the plain glazed. They believed that they should have the honor of being first. In the other box were the chocolate chip cookies laughing at the oatmeal cookies. The chocolate cookie carried with it, extra baked-in gifts of M&Ms, red and green.

Soon, it became box against box. The doughnuts against the cookies. All of them vying to be the first chosen come Christmas morning. I believe I can hear the muffled yelling going back and forth in my ears until I slide off to sleep. Ultimately, all of their arguing about who went when didn't really matter. In the middle of the night, the dog chose instead of me. And as always, he's not all that picky.

Sambuca

Black only, not white. Served in a clear goblet, warmed over a candle and turned slowly to capture the flavor of the coffee beans floating in the precious liquid. I watched it being rotated by the bartender as I sat in the giant plush leather chair that occupies a space in the private club next to the bar. I usually have several after a good meal and smile contentedly like the overly satisfied man that I am.

As it was getting late in the hour, people began leaving, and ultimately, it was just me alone in the room. After a short while, the sambuca did what it does, and I saw the trophy case door swing open on its own. Many of the small gold men began to leap from atop the individual trophies they stood upon and began to land out onto the green felt of the pool table.

The smooth and polished baseball men began to play a few innings around a makeshift diamond using cue chalk to mark the bases. I sat back and watched from my sole seat in the front row bleachers, cheering them on. When they had finished, they waved, some tipping their hats in appreciation, and made their way back to the tops of the trophies where they belonged.

It didn't seem like a very long time before I was roused by the clanking of glasses and dishes in the kitchen and smelled the aroma of fresh brewed coffee coming from the morning crew. One of the guys came out and handed me a hot mug, my now seemingly normal wake up steam facial in a cup.

I knew it was time to finally go home but not before I made sure that I was alone when I picked up the tiny gold bat that was laying on the pool table and placed it back into the hole of the loosely formed hands of the player on the trophy that left it behind.

I will be back tonight for more perfectly cooked steak and an evening finished off by many warm sambucas. I also will once again wait until everyone is gone to see if by some chance the little jockeys perched upon their shiny silver horses in the trophy case decide to come down as they have before, jumping onto the "grass track" of the pool table to stage an impromptu horserace.

Hope

We noticed from the beginning that she had no fear of animals, and they had no fear of her.

It started innocently enough when she was very young and stumbled into an ant pile. The ants quickly crawled all over her but never bit her.

Wasps and bees would land on her daily but never sting.

Birds continually flew down to sit on her shoulder and sing to her.

Every dog she saw became fiercely protective of her, and cats would cry for her to pet them whenever she was near one.

We stopped going to the zoo. The animals stared at her and followed her inside their habitats until she was out of their sight, then they would all cry out as if they were wounded. It continued to escalate.

I brought her fishing once, and fish just jumped into the boat. Dozens and dozens at a time threatening to sink us. We stopped going fishing, too, but then we couldn't even go near the water because they would swim out and onto the land squirming their way through the grass toward us trying to be near her.

Once, not long ago, I witnessed a large group of butterflies form a shield above her when she was momentarily exposed to the harsh sunlight of the afternoon. It has all been so very strange, but I think I am beginning to understand why they all watch out for her.

She is four years old today and has never been sick a day in her life. I believe that perhaps even the smallest creatures are also looking after her. Even the extremely tiny ones that we can't see. Even the ones that made me terribly ill recently, that is, until she came over and held my hand.

Bill

He always comes to me in times of need, in times where I am lonely or feeling especially down. I can hear his claws rapidly tapping on the wooden floor with a rushed abandon, racing around the corner, and jumping up on the couch next to me, licking my face as I reach over to pet his thick brown fur.

There is a great comfort that comes with his visits, but there is also great disappointment. You see, there is no giant bowl of food or water on the floor in the kitchen for him. There is no leash hanging on a hook waiting for me to attach it to his collar as we trek out for an evening walk.

Those things always come to my mind as he jumps down from my lap and slowly fades away into the evening air. His visits are brief but very welcome. Each time, it is such an odd thing to watch him slowly disappear as he stares into my eyes.

When he made his first appearance, I assumed that he accidentally got into the house. I thought I might have left the door ajar as he came tearing his way around the corner through the kitchen doorway. I first presumed that he belonged to a neighbor, so naturally, I looked at his tag. It said his name was Bill; the phone number was none that I recognized, but it also said that he was mine, that I was his owner. Since that day, it has been a waiting game for me.

And I keep doing just that: waiting. Waiting for the day when my number is somehow changed by a new service or that I might be transferred and move to another place and receive that phone number. That will be the moment I will know it's time to begin to look for him.

Maybe he will be in a shelter somewhere anxious for me to save him. Maybe he will walk up to me in a parking lot all cold and hungry. Whenever and however it will happen, I know for certain that his name is Bill, and I will have the bowls and the leash and the food waiting for him.

And it will be so wonderful to have my canine friend with me permanently. Until then, I will cherish the time I have when he fades in and then fades out, and maybe figure out along the way why I named him Bill.

He Left for Parts Unknown

is usually reserved for characters of no significance to the story. Ones who disappear and are never heard from again, ones you never give a second thought.

I only mention it because today, for once, it was nice to leave the field I am usually sitting in while staring up at the clouds, continuously dreaming up useless stories.

I will tell you that it doesn't look like a herd of cows when you see the clouds from above. I can say that because today, I finally decided it was time to fly. I spread my arms out and began to wave until I lifted off the ground enough to get caught up in a breeze which took me off into the sky.

A hawk came over to check and see what I was all about, see what it was that was occupying his normally exclusive air space. He squawked at me then went on his way, seemingly satisfied that I was of no importance.

And then he did as all insignificant characters in stories do, he left for parts unknown, as I, too, will now do.

About The Author

Robert "Bob" Medina is a retired firefighter, chef, and transplanted New Orleanian. He got his cooking chops at home with his family and in the firehouse where he was the cook, putting to good use all he had learned from his family.

Robert lives in Northwest Florida with his wife, Lori.

www.ingramcontent.com/pod-product-compliance
Lightning Source LLC
Chambersburg PA
CBHW030328100526
44592CB00010B/612